Greek Mythology

The Myths of Ancient Greece from the Origin of the Cosmos and the Appearance of the Titans to the Time of Gods and Men. Invincible Heroes, Evil Gods, Monsters and Memorable Feats.

Aula Magna

© Copyright 2023 Aula Magna - All Rights Reserved

The contents of this book may not be reproduced, duplicated or transmitted without the written permission of the author or publisher.

Under no circumstances shall any legal fault or liability be attributed to the publisher or author for damages, repairs, or monetary losses due to the information contained in thisbook, directly or indirectly.

Legal notice

This book is copyrighted. This book is for personal use only. You may not modify, distribute, sell, use, quote, orparaphrase any part, or the content within this book, without the consent of the author or publisher.

Notice of disclaimer

Please note that the information in this document is for educational and entertainment purposes only. Every effort has been made to present accurate, up-to-date and reliable, complete information. No warranty of any kind is stated or implied. Readers acknowledge that the author makes no commitment to provide legal, financial, medical, or professional advice

Table of Contents

Introduction

Chapter 1

Creation of the world according to Greek mythology

- 1.1 The Chaos………………………………… 9
- 1.2 Uranus and Gaia……………………….10
- 1.3 The threads of destiny…………………….12
- 1.4 The descendants of Pontus……………….14
- 1.5 Cronus and the rise of the Titans………….15
- 1.6 The birth of Zeus……………………….20
- 1.7 The Fall of Cronus……………………….24
- 1.8 Age of men………………………………35

Chapter 2

The Greek Heroes

- 2.1 Bellerophon……………………………….41
- 2.2 Heracles………………………………...45
- 2.3 Perseus…………………………………….59
- 2.4 Theseus…………………………………….65
- 2.5 Jason………………………………………77

Chapter 3

<u>Greek deities</u>

- 3.1 Zeus………………………………………………………100
- 3.2 Poseidon…….…………………………………………....102
- 3.3 Hades……..…………………………………………..….103
- 3.4 Hera……..………………………………………………..103
- 3.5 Demeter……..…………………………………………....104
- 3.6 Hestia……..……………………………………………....105
- 3.7 Apollo…..………………………………………………...105
- 3.8 Artemis……………………………………………….…..106
- 3.9 Hermes…..………………………………………….……107
- 3.10 Dionys……..…. …………………………………….….109
- 3.11 Ares ……………………………………………….……110
- 3.12 Aphrodite……………………………………………….111
- 3.13 Athena…..……………………………………………....112
- 3.14 Hephaestus...…………………………………………….114

Chapter 4

<u>Greek myths</u>

- 4.1 The chains of Prometheus...……………………………….116
- 4.2 Pandora's Box...…………....…………………………123
- 4.3 The 12 Labors of Heracles...…………………………….127
- 4.4 Eros and Psyche...…..…………………………… 146
- 4.5 Apollo and Daphne ………………………………….150

Introduction

Hellenic mythology consists mainly of a set of legends and tales concerning various deities. It developed entirely between the 9th and 8th centuries BCE, a period when Homer's Iliad and Odyssey and Hesiod's Theogony appeared. Greek mythology has some specific peculiarities: the gods present human aspects and sensibilities and, with the exception of ancient religions such as Hinduism or Judaism, it does not present revelations or teachings of a spiritual nature. Moreover, the customs and practices of worship were quite varied, despite having no text of a sacred nature and no institutional structures such as clergy. According to tradition, the Greek deities dwelt on Mount Olympus in Thessaly, where they formed a hierarchical society under their hegemony and authority; at any rate, they could move independently throughout the world. Some deities were associated with three major kingdoms: the sky, the sea and the earth.

The twelve main deities, usually referred to as "Olympians," were Zeus, Hera, Hephaestus, Athena, Apollo, Artemis, Ares, Aphrodite, Hestia, Hermes, Demeter, and Poseidon. Hades was not generally considered a member of 'Olympus since he reigned in the Underworld, where he resided with his wife Persephone.

Dionysus, God of wine and natural life, was frequently surrounded by secondary deities such as satyrs, centaurs and nymphs; numerous celebrations were dedicated to him, and in some regions, he even achieved the same fame as Zeus.

Greek mythology accentuated the fragility of human beings as opposed to the magniloquent and fearsome forces of nature. The Greeks believed that the gods were eternal and thought that their own lives and natural events derived entirely from the will of the gods; generally, the ties between the gods and human beings were cordial, but the deities could inflict severe punishments on humans who displayed an impermissible attitude, such as complacency or unbridled ambition, or who displayed excessive prosperity.

In Greece, mythology was interconnected with every aspect of life: all cities were dedicated to a god or set of deities, for whom residents erected shrines. At celebrations, periodically dedicated to the deities, which took place under the supervision of the city governors, poets told or sang stories and tales, through which the Greeks learned the history of the deities. They also did this through oral transmission in their families. Moreover, various areas of the home were dedicated to deities; for example, an altar of Zeus could be found in the garden, while Estia was honored in the heart of the living room, near the hearth.

Although the Greeks had no religious organization on an official level, they did possess some places of worship to worship: among them was Delphi, which was consecrated to Apollo. Inside temples were oracles, which wayfarers consulted to find out the future. Each religious site consisted of a set of presbyters who also constituted the authorities of the community and who interpreted the words of the deities but had no particularly relevant knowledge or faculties. In addition to ceremonies, the Greeks often presented sacrifices to the gods, usually animals such as mutton. Hellenic mythology likely evolved from the primitive religions of the indigenous people of Crete. Over time, from an initial animism, these beliefs developed into a sequence of myths involving objects of nature, animals, and deities with human features, parts of which flowed into ancient Greek mythology. It was the ancient Greeks themselves who gave some elucidation about the development of their mythology.

During the 5th century BCE, the great philosopher Prodicus of Ceos argued that the gods were personifications of natural events such as the sun, moon, winds, and waters; Herodotus, a scholar of Greek history who also lived in the 5th century BCE, believed that many Greek ceremonials had been handed down from the Egyptians.

With the development of Greek civilization, especially under the Hellenistic period, which began around 323 BCE, mythology began to change as well. New doctrines and influences from neighboring peoples caused a gradual change in religious beliefs, while keeping intact the substantial particularities and legends of Greek deities.

Chapter 1

Creation of the world according to Greek mythology

1.1 The Chaos

At the origin of everything according to Greek mythology was Chaos. Chaos was seen as a chasm, a dark and formless mass from where everything originated. Originally the appearance of nature had no form. There was no heaven, no earth, and no sun, but a formless abyss in which all the elements were mixed, a multitude of different microbes, and mismatched things. Out of this Chaos was born Gaia, Mother Earth endowed with a huge bosom, a safe place for all mortals and immortals. Shortly thereafter, the stormy Tartarus was born, a horrible underground darkness, completely devoid of any light, that lurked in the meanders of the Earth. Later Gaia generated Uranus alone, a sky studded with stars and high mountains. Out of Chaos was born the strongest of all deities: Eros, love, the most wonderful of all the Celestials. (With the birth of Zeus, Eros will lose the title of strongest deity).
Later from Chaos also arose Erebus, oppressive darkness of the abyssal depths, and Nyx, the black-winged night.

1.2   Uranus and Gaia

As we said before, the earth goddess Gaia had given birth to Uranus, the sky god covered with stars
Uranus was the first ruler of the cosmos; clinging to Gaia, he impregnated her by casting fertilizing raindrops on her.
From Gaia sprang first Ocean, the river that surrounds all the landmasses; and after him came Coeo, Chryo, Hyperion, and Iapetus.

Subsequently, six daughters were born: Theia, Rhea, Temis, Mnemosyne, Phoebe (of the golden garland) and the beautiful Thetis. After the birth of the latter, eventually, Kronos was born, the youngest but meanest of his line.

Next, Gaia and Uranus begat three Cyclopes with noble hearts, boundless strength and ingenious cunning. Their names were Bronte, the "thunderous," Sterope, the "flashing," and Arges, the "violent heart." They resembled the other immortal gods in all respects, but possessed one large round eye in the middle of their foreheads. Other sons were born from the earth Gaia and the sky Uranus: Coto, Briareo and Gige, beings of extreme arrogance. They were called Ecantochei, the hundred-armed giants.

Uranus, however, felt revulsion for the children born of his union with Gaia; he considered them a real threat. So when they were born, he sent them back into the belly of the made determined not to let the world know about the hideous lineage. Gaia, he grieved very much for the choice made by Uranus and decided to take revenge by devising a plan as cunning as it was wicked. She built a great scythe to ambush her hated husband and stated, addressing her children, " My dear children, whom I begat with an unclean and merciless being, if you will listen to me you will have the opportunity to take revenge on your father, who first plotted behind your back."

Thus, the earth goddess expressed herself, but all the Parthians were seized with great awe, and none dared to speak. At that point, taking courage, Kronos exposed himself, and abandoning fear, he supported the reasons of his mother Gaia.

"I guarantee that I will bring your plan to fruition, my dear mother." Overjoyed at hearing such words, Gaia gave the scythe to Kronos and told him to hide in the tall grass.

Night came, and Uranus, eager to lie with Gaia, lay down on the ground. Cronus, who was lurking in the tall grass, clutched his scythe and struck Uranus' penis with enormous force, cutting it in two.

Shamed and banished to the farthest region of the cosmos, Uranus cursed his sons, calling them Titans for the first time, since, according to him, they had had no qualms about killing their father. According to Uranus, they had made a huge mistake and would pay the consequences sooner or later.

From that time, however, Heaven no longer approached Earth to receive the nightly embrace.

From the blood of Uranus, collected in the bosom of Mother Earth Gaia, other bizarre beings were born in the meantime. The mighty Erinyes, better known as the Furies: Megaera, Tisiphone and Alekto, the "jealous," the "vengeful," and the "implacable." Old, dark-skinned winged witches with hair mutated into snakes, who persecuted all those who were guilty of grave faults and murders, especially against relatives and blood relatives.

From this blood was made in particular the blood of the Giants. Attired in their bronze armor, and with very long spears in their hands, they would wage war against all deities. Also born were the nymphs of the ash trees, called Meliads. Perennially sad and dissatisfied creatures, they offered their tough and indestructible wood to make spears and javelins.

1.3 The threads of destiny

The new cosmos had been born in the presence of a horrible murder: the revolt of Kronos against his father Uranus. From there on, suffering and violence would be an integral part of the world.

In the days of Kronos, the dark Nyx, without lying with anyone, gave birth to many dark and evil deities: Moros the doom, Ker the black misfortune, Thanatos the death, Hypnos the sleep, and with the latter the Oneiroi, the unwanted guests of nightmares.

Subsequently, he created Momos the guilt and Oizys the misery. And again Nemesis the dreadful vengeance, a scourge to mortal men, and Apate, the deception, Philotes the friendship, Geras the ruinous old age, Eris the violent- hearted discord, and, finally, Keres, the ruthless in giving punishment.

These are beings that symbolize the darkest and most hateful parts of life, which humans try to evade in every way.

Prominent among the descendants of Nyx was Eris, the discordant with a violent heart, who worshipped war and contestation. No mortal particularly worshipped her. This deity was well present among humans from ancient times.

Eris, in turn, created Ponos, the excruciating pain, Lethe, the oblivion, Limos, the famine, and with it the Algoi, the sorrows that cause tears, the Hysminai and the Makhai, the contentions and wars, the Phonoi and the Androktasiai, the crimes and murders, and finally Neikos the contention and Pseudos the lies, and with it the Logoi and the Amphilogoi, the righteous speeches and the ambiguous speeches.

And again, Dysnomia the anarchy and Ate the delusion, malignant goddesses who acted in cahoots, and finally Horkos the oath, which caused misfortunes among men when they deliberately betrayed their promise and perjured themselves.

The Daughters of Nyx also included the Moirai, beings of occult power from which even the deities could not escape; every day they wove, measured and cut the threads of every living being's destiny, deciding its good and evil. There were three of them and their names were Klotho, Lakhesis and Atropos. They persecuted men and gods based on their misdeeds; no one was exempt from their jurisdiction. They harbored unrelenting rage and fury against those they had to judge.

They went in search of men and gods who had been guilty of horrendous crimes in order to punish them by inflicting horrible punishments on them.

Their power was so archaic that even Zeus, the next ruler of the heavens, had no right to change their rulings.

Also, daughters of Nyx (although according to others they would be daughters of Zeus and Themis), the Hesperides were the nymphs of twilight. They lived in the far west, on a 'little island across the Ocean River. There were three Hesperides: Aigle, the "radiant," Erytheia, the "red," and Hespera, the " fast." In their fantastic garden, with the complicity of the adder Ladon, they stored the golden apples of immortality.

1.4   The descendants of Pontus.

After the dismemberment of Uranus, Gaia turned her attentions to Pontus. From that union came the creatures of the sea--but also some of the most frightening creatures of the Hellenic myths.

From the union of the broad-breasted land and the salty sea, there first arose Nereus, the old man of the sea, sincere and benign, a source of justice and mild counsel.

But terrible creatures were also spawned from this marriage: the giant Thaumas, the wonder of the sea, and the mighty Phorcys, and Ceto with a beautiful face, and Eurybia, who possessed a heart stronger than metal.

Old Nereus, who was ruler of the seas even before Poseidon, later married Doris, daughter of Oceanus, and she made him father of all the sea nymphs. From Nereus, the spotless god, fifty daughters were born: the Nereids.

The immense Thaumas, the sea wonder, married Elektra, another of Ocean's daughters, who begat Iris, the swift goddess of rainbows, who unites earth and sky.

She later begat the Harpies, the winged goddesses with long curly hair who were abductors of people. Their names were Aello and Ocypete (although others say there were three, with the addition of Kelaino), and later represented with women's heads on birds of prey.

Out of the marriage of Phorcys to his sister Ceto, came a series of frightening creatures: the Gorgons. These creatures were equipped with a body covered with scales like that of reptiles and possessed live snakes instead of hair. They were called Stheno, Euryale and Medusa and held the tremendous power to pity anyone unfortunate enough to cross their gaze.

Although Stheno and Euryale possessed the power of immortality, only Medusa could be eliminated. One of the Greeks' most adored heroes, the valiant Perseus, killed the Gorgon by severing her head. The winged horse Pegasus and the golden-sworded knight, Chrysaurus, were born from Medusa's severed neck.

From the unfortunate marriage between the two sea deities, the Graeae were also born. They were the "Graeae," whose appearance was perhaps less frightening than that of the Gorgon sisters, but who, in any case, represented at least an unusual sight to men who dared to visit them at the ends of the world. They were Pemphredo, with the shining peplos, and Enyo with the ravening peplos. Others added a third: Deino. They were born old and white-haired; they also shared an eye and a tooth, which they took turns exchanging.

Equally the daughter of Phorcys and Ceto-though many others point to a different lineage-was the terrifying Echidna, who possessed a rather savage heart, half bright-eyed maiden and half viper, whose progeny was no less threatening than the others. As the last-born of Ceto and Phorcys there was the serpent Ládon; born to watch over the golden apples of the Hesperides.

Echidna is said to have married Typhon, son of Tartarus and Gaia. He was a disloyal and aggressive monster, disrespectful of any law. The two lived in a craggy underground cave in the land of the Arimoi. Here Echidna begat a hideous offspring with hearts filled with hatred.

First was born Orthrus, the monstrous dog of Geryon, son of Chrysaor. Dog and herdsman would be killed by Heracles.

The second was Cerberus, the bronze-voiced dog, guardian of the fallen kingdom. His torso was covered with serpents and had fifty heads (although others claim only three). The third was the Hydra of Lerna, a spectral nine-headed dragon, which Hera begat because she harbored an unbearable animosity toward Heracles.

Then she gave birth to the Chimera, a despicable three- headed monster: one of a lion, one of a goat, and one of a snake. The latter was defeated by the brave Bellerophon.

Later, conjoining with her own firstborn, the dog Orthrus, Echidna conceived Sphinx, a half-lion, half-woman creature who tormented passersby by subjecting them to riddles and eating those who could not answer them.

Later Echidna gave birth to the Lion of Nemea, a fierce, savage and horrible, beast, also doomed to be defeated by Heracles. The father of this was the hound Orthrus; for others, however, it was Typhon.

But other terrible descendants are still attributed to Echidna, with the complicity of Typhon. According to some, she was the mother of Ladon the dragon, who guarded the apples of the Hesperides, and also of the Dragon of Colchi, guardian of the Golden Fleece. According to others, she would be the mother of the eagle that devoured Prometheus' liver (although this is said to have been the daughter of Tartarus and Gaia, or to have been specially forged by Hephaestus).

Others claim that Echidna was the mother of Scylla, who was half girl and half dog and was later eliminated by Heracles. While others claim that she procreated the Crommian sow Phaia, who would in turn be eliminated by Theseus, and still others claim that Echidna begat a certain Gorgo, father of the Gorgons.

It is said that the tremendous Echidna used to attack and plunder wayfarers. Argos, the hundred-eyed behemoth, caught her by surprise in her sleep and eliminated her, making the world free of her presence.

1.5 Cronus and the rise of the Titans

The second cosmos, dominated by Kronos, was marked by the reign of the giant Titans, descendants of Uranus and Gaia. From their descendants came another divine generation: the sun, moon, rosy-fingered dawn, river gods and sea nymphs. It was the golden age.

After routing Uranus, Kronos imposed his sovereignty over the universe. The second cosmic order was thus marked by the rule of the Titans. Mighty and universal creatures of colossal stature.

As has been mentioned earlier, there were six males (Oceanus, Coeo, Chryo, Hyperion, Hyapetus, and Chronos) and six females (Theia, Rhea, Themis, Mnemosyne, Phoebe, and Thetys). The oldest of the Titans was Ocean, who surrounded the world with his waves. Joining with his sister Thetys, he begat the lineage of rivers, Potamoi: from Nilus to Alpheus, from Eridanus to Strymon, and to the divine Scamander flowing beside the gates of Troy. There were, the story goes, more than 3,000 rivers that, drawing their waters from Oceanus, traverse the earth.

Oceanus and Thetys also conceived the offspring of the Oceanids, the nymphs living in the dark depths. These included Peitho, Admete, Elektra, Doris, Ourania, Metis, Calypso (the destination of hearts' desire), and, again, Styx, the most distinguished among them all.

Doris took to wife Nereus, son of Pontus and Gaia, and thus begat the sea nymphs. Elektra, on the other hand, married Thaumas, also the son of Pontus and Gaia, and made him the father of Iris, goddess of the rainbow, and the Harpies. Hyperion conjoined with his sister Theia and procreated Helios, the magnificent sun, and Selene, the shining moon, and the beautiful Eos, the pink-lipped aurora.

Crius united with Eurybia, daughter of Pontus and Gaia. Having fallen in love with her, he begat Astraeus, Pallas and Perses.

Astraeus became the husband of Eos, goddess of the dawn, who bore winds of impetuous character, such as the shining Zephyrus, the west wind, and Borea, which blew from the north, Notus, which brought fog and rain from the south. Also born from that marriage were Hesperos, deities of awakening, and the Astra, the shining stars surrounding the firmament. Pallas instead united in marriage with Styx and begat, in his palace, Zeus. Nike the victory, Kratos the power, and Bia the strength. will forever be Zeus' bodyguards.

The novice ruler of the universe, Cronus, in bad faith, married Rhea, from whom splendid children were born: Hestia, Demeter, Hera (the goddess of the golden slipper), Hades (with a cruel heart), and Poseidon, the Ennosigaios, " who was able to shake the earth" with deep echoes.

1.6 The birth of Zeus

The new king of the universe was hidden in a cave, safe from the eyes of the wicked ruler.

According to many, Zeus was born in Parrhasia, in southern Arcadia. Here is Mount Lykaion, which the Arcadians called Olympus; there was an area called Crete, and the Arcadians claimed that this was none other than the island of Crete, the birthplace of Zeus.

On the highest peak of the mountain, from where the entire Peloponnese could be seen, the Arcadians raised a mound of earth, a kind of altar dedicated to Zeus Lykaios. To the god was also dedicated an enclosure, located nearby, where no one, man or animal, could approach. It was forbidden for anyone to enter this enclosure. If anyone, violating the law, entered it, he would inevitably die within a year.

The Arcadians, as we have recounted, claimed that Rhea secretly headed to a rather hidden place on Mount Lykaion specifically to give birth to Zeus.

Three nymphs came to help her: Neda, Theisoa and Hagno. As soon as Rhea gave birth to the child, she immediately went to look for a stream to wash it. But in those days no rivers or streams ran through those lands. At this point Rea gave a sharp blow to the mountain and said:

"Gaia, dear earth I need your help to bring your work into the world in the best possible way".

Immediately, the rock opened wide and a torrent of water gushed from the chasm. Rhea washed the infant in it and entrusted it to Neda, the eldest of the three nymphs, to take it as soon as possible to Crete, to hide it from the eyes of Cronus. The nymph obeyed, and Rhea gratefully gave her name to the newly-flowing river.

As soon as Neda arrived in Crete with her newborn in her arms, the umbilical cord detached from the child. This happened in Thenae, in a valley near Knossos, and the inhabitants still call that place Omphalos. Later, the baby was taken to Mount Dikti, where it was taken into the arms of the Meliae, the nymphs of the ash trees who lived on the mountain. At this place, the baby was placed in a golden cradle and cuddled by Adrasteia, daughter of King Melisseus.

At that point the nymphs brought him a goat named Amalthea so that Zeus could drink her milk, and then came the bee Panakridos, to feed the little infant with her honey.

The Korybantes began a fighting dance around the cradle, to mask the newborn's groans , so that his father Kronos would not find him.

At that time, ancient Melisseus ruled over Crete. He was the first to develop worship rites and offer sacrifices to the deities. Rhea entrusted the child to her daughters, the nymphs Adrasteia and Ida, but the two maidens had no milk, as we have already explained, and for this reason they placed near the child the goat Amalthea, who had just given birth to two kids, and it was, therefore she who suckled the baby Zeus. Later, in gratitude, the god took Amalthea and her two goats among the stars. According to others, Melisseus' daughters were named Amalthea and Melissa; the former fed Zeus with goat's milk, the latter with honey.

Zeus grew up quietly in Crete, under the watchful attention of the two nymphs. Adrasteia gave him, for fun, a wonderful ball, made of golden circles and covered with a blue vault. Once thrown, it left a bright furrow in the air, as if it were a comet star.

When Kronos noticed that Rhea had just given birth to the newborn, he commanded her to hand it over to him immediately.

Rhea wrapped a stone in a cloth, as if it were an infant, and gave it to her husband. Without realizing the deception, Kronos swallowed it. His teeth, knocking against the stone, split. Still he was persuaded that he had mauled his last heir.

Rhéa's deception, unfortunately, could not be sustained for long. The moment Kronos realized that he had been cheated and realizing that his son was still alive, he began to search everywhere for baby Zeus in order to dispose of him.

It was then that his nurses, the titans Themis and Amalthea, to whom Rhea had entrusted the child, hid him on the island of Crete. To prevent his father from seeing him, Amalthea placed him on a cradle suspended from the branch of a tree, so that he was neither on land, nor in the sea, nor in the sky, and, therefore, escaped Kronos's patrols. To cover the child's weeping, he had fighters come, to whom he gave bronze spears and shields, ordering them to dance around the tree and slam them into each other. They were the Korybantes.

As we have stated, Amalthea was a goat. She is said to have had two beautiful horns, erect and curved. One horn broke off in a scuffle with a tree. Amalthea picked it up and, after garnishing it with herbs and filling it with fruit, gave it to Zeus.

From then on, this horn took on the ability to fill itself with fruit, becoming the horn of plenty.

Some years later, as soon as Zeus waged war against the Titans, he dressed himself in the skin of Aex. A soothsayer warned him that only in this way could he achieve victory. Having regained his own kingdom, Zeus collected the goat's bones and restored her life by placing her among the stars.

This skin, called "aegis," adorned with Medusa's head, was later given to Athena, who used it to cover her own shield.

1.7 The Fall of Cronus

Once Zeus rallied several allies, he finally opposed Kronos and the hegemony of the Titans. It was only the beginning of a very long battle between two opposing worlds, which could only be resolved by releasing the powers that Uranus had confined to Tartarus...

As time passed, Zeus grew strong and healthy on the island of Crete, until he became convinced that the time had come to stand against his father, Cronus. The supremacy of the Titans was marked by violence and cruelty, but the oracle of Mother Earth Gaia, she who had many names and one form, said:

"There is no need to be either strong or mighty; the most cunning will be sovereign."

Cunning was never lacking in Zeus. He could also rely on the help of Meti the Oceanid, daughter of Oceanus, the most cunning and intelligent of all the gods and mortals, who would also become his first companion. It is said that it was she who delivered a potion to Kronos, which forced the ruler of the Titans to reject what he had ingested.

Still according to others, it was Gaia herself who deceived Kronos, forcing him to regurgitate his previously devoured children.

In each case, Kronos first rejected the stone that had been swallowed as the last, instead of the newborn Zeus. Next, Kronos rejected, one after another, Poseidon, Hades, Hera, Demeter, and Estia. These emerged alive, and adult, from their father's stomach.

In the company of his brothers and sisters, Zeus climbed to the top of

Mount Olympus in northern Thessaly. He announced that anyone who was willing to fight by his side against Kronos and the Titans would keep the tributes he already had. And he added that all those whom Kronos had stripped of their rights would obtain from him the tributes that the law required.

The immortals were then divided between those who supported Cronus and those who supported Zeus' supremacy. Reaching Olympus first was the river goddess Styx, the last daughter of Oceanus. Along with her were two of her sons, Kratos the "power" and Bia the "strength." Zeus placed the two young men beside himself. From that day on, they became his most faithful bodyguards. There was no way Zeus would travel without Kratos and Bia. They were always by his side; their place was always beside his throne. On the Styx itself, Zeus bestowed magnificent gifts and established the great covenant between the gods.

Cronus took sides with his brothers Coeus, Crius, Hyperion and Iapetus on Mount Othrys in southern Thessaly. Only Oceanus remained neutral in his home at the edge of the world. The Titans' strategy was based on the use of cruel violence, but Iapetus' son, the cunning Prometheus, tried to bring them back to reason. He reminded them that Gaia had sanctioned the victory not of the mightiest, but of the cleverest and wisest.

The Titans, however, did not heed his warning. Prometheus then decided to switch sides with Zeus.

For ten years, the two different divine lineages faced each other in terrible clashes. To this bitter contention, there seemed to be no conclusion or solution. Nor did the clashes benefit either faction. The end of the war loomed remote and and uncertain.

The oracle of the earthly goddess Gaia predicted Zeus' victory, provided he took as allies those whom Uranus, because of his wickedness, had imprisoned in Tartarus. Envious of their strength and appearance, the Hecatonchi, the giants with a hundred arms, had been chained in the bowels of the earth, at the edge of the planet.

The angry-hearted Cyclopes had suffered the same fate: Brontes, Steropes and Arges were locked under the earth. Zeus therefore went as far as Tartarus and, after killing Kampe, the monster who guarded Uranus' captives, loosened the Hecatonchians and Cyclopes from the bonds their father had imposed on them.

Transported to Mount Olympus, the Hecatoncheans and Cyclopes were refreshed with ambrosia, the same food that the deities took. That meal instilled ardor and courage in their hearts.

So Zeus turned to these and said, " Lend me your ear, magnificent sons of Gaia and Uranus. We have been fighting against the Titans for a long time; I thought, therefore, that you having returned to the light by my choice, having suffered so long in the dark darkness, you should show me gratitude by fighting by my side against Kronos. Your strength is essential to winning this war."

Cottus replied, on behalf of his brothers: Lord, do not tell us things we already know; we know that in you dwell wisdom and cunning. We know that you have prevented your brothers from the devastating rage of Cronus. And we know that we have been delivered from 'darkness by your will. Therefore, with an unflinching conscience and a shrewd brain, we will fight at your own side against the Titans, supporting you even in the toughest battles.

All the deities praised his intervention eager to see them fight against Kronos and the Titans.

The Cyclopes got busy and handed over to Zeus the thunder, flaming lightning, and thunderbolt they had previously kept hidden.

To Poseidon they gave the trident and to Hades the helmet that makes one invisible.

The war began again with unprecedented violence. On one side were the Titans; on the other side were the many who had been created by Kronos and their allies.

The mighty Hecatonics lined up in front of the enemy and, rolling a hundred arms sprouting from their own shoulders, began to throw huge boulders at them. On the opposite side, the Titans quickly reinforced their ranks and, in turn, showed what strength and arrogance they were made of. The struggle was so tremendous that the sea vibrated, the earth rumbled and the sky grew gloomy. Mount Olympus itself faltered under the siege of the Titans, and the tremors of that unspeakable tumult reached as far as Tartarus. The two armies faced each other causing an indescribable uproar, and their cries reached as far as the starry sky.

Zeus could not hold back his anger. His heart filled with rage, he revealed all his anger and power. Grasping the lightning, foraged by the Cyclopes, he descended from Olympus in the form of lightning. Thunderbolts fell from the sky, the earth rumbled, the forests burned, and the ocean currents boiled.

Thunder, lightning and thunderbolts, hurled like arrows, caused shouts and cries from both sides; there was such a din that it seemed as if the sky was about to rush down to the earth, or that the earth was rising up to collide with the sky. It was as if Uranus and Gaia were about to be reunited in their embrace; but this great uproar was caused only by the immortals fighting among themselves.

Subsequently, the battle turned into degradation. Blinded by lightning, overwhelmed by fiery winds, shattered by boulders hurled down from the sky, the Titans were annihilated.

Finally felled, the Titans were surrounded by terrible chains. It was the Hecatoncheans who dragged them underground, to a remote place on the earth's surface and far from the heavens: Tartarus. A dark and distressing place that even the gods hated. Raging winds would immediately pounce on anyone who passed through those gates, dragging them from one blizzard to another.

There, in the gloomy, dark mist, the Titans had been imprisoned, in a dismal land at the edge of the world. A bronze fence surrounded that place. On that wall, Poseidon placed bronze doors, which, however, the Titans were not allowed to pass through. There lived Gige, Cottus and the magnanimous Briareus, faithful guardians of Zeus.

Not far to the west stretched the terrible home of Nyx, the dark night, surrounded by shining clouds. Nearby, Nyx and Hemera met regularly, night and day, who took turns in passing through the bronze portal, one to descend, the other to travel along the land and sea. The sons of Nyx also resided here: Hypnos the sleep and Thanatos the fatal death. Of these, the one traveled along the land and the wide seabed; the other, with a heart of iron and a soul of bronze, held forever in his possession anyone who grasped him. Styx also dwelt nearby, in an illustrious dwelling, covered with rocks, resting on silver pillars erected toward the sky. In front was the house of the underworld, which Hades would one day occupy with his queen.

But it was the sons of Iapetus who suffered the harshest treatment. Atlas, who many believe led the Titans into battle, was confined to the west, near the Hesperides Islands, exactly in front of Nyx's house.

And there, standing erect with untiring head and arms, he was condemned to hold up the vault of heaven. His brother, the arrogant Menoetius, was electrocuted by lightning and plunged into the gloomy Erebus. The cunning Prometheus, who had also rescued Zeus during war, was Chained-but for other reasons-to the rocks of Caucasus. As for the wretched Epimetheus, he suffered no torture, although he had been the cause of eternal punishment for the entire human race...

The fate of the titanesses-Theia, Themis, Mnemosyne, and Phoebe-was milder. Others claim that Kronos was confined to the "Islands of the Blessed," located in the far west, near Oceanus. It was a fermented land, producing fruit in abundance at least three times a year. There, seated on a throne next to Rhea, Kronos ruled the heroic ranks of the Bronze Age.

Others claim that Kronos was exiled to the island of Ogigia, five days' sail off Britannia. He lay asleep in a deep cave, inside a golden rock, while Briareus stood beside him. Sleep, many claim, was the only torment Zeus inflicted on him. As birds flew to the top of the rock to bring him ambrosia, the island was pervaded by a perfume that wafted as if from a spring.

Demons assisted and served Chronos as his faithful servants during the golden age of the titans. They were endowed with prophetic virtues. Prophecies concerning serious matters were announced to Kronos only in dreams. What Zeus foretold; Kronos saw in a dream. In contrast, Orpheus claimed that Kronos was trapped thanks to a honey bowl. Such deception would have been advised to Zeus by Nyx. In those days, wine had not yet been produced and feeling fulfilled in the same way, Kronos fell asleep after ingesting honey.

Kronos dozed off. Then Zeus imprisoned his father and castrated him, just as Kronos did to Uranus himself.

Rather, the Latins claimed that Chronos took refuge in Latium, identifying him as Saturnus, deity of agriculture.

As for the rock thrown by Kronos, Zeus placed it in the valleys below the yokes of Parnassus, so that it would become a warning for the future, a sign for mortals. This place was the fulcrum of the kingdom: Two eagles (or two swans), departing from the extreme tips of the earth and heading inland, met right there, by the supreme Pytho, where within a year the temple of Delphoi would be born.

Such a place became the most sacred in all of Hellas, and there the boulder placed by Zeus was appreciated and celebrated throughout the centuries as "omphalós," the navel of the world.

On either side stood two golden eagles in memory of the effort undertaken by the two birds.

Delphi became the home of a distinguished soothsayer. It was Gaia, goddess of the earth, who uttered her first prophecy in that same temple (she had actually been the oracle that guided Zeus' rise to his sovereignty). Later, it would be the titan Themis, her daughter, who would guard the oracle.

Zeus therefore got rid of the Titans, gathered their ungovernable and untamable power and distributed it with his brothers and sisters, laying the foundation for a new ancestral kingdom and order. Through a series of unions, he scattered his seed and divinity as well among mortals giving birth to a great many of his "bastard" children. Dike, guardian goddess of the laws, and Irene, goddess of benevolence, were born, and from their union with Mnemosyne, the golden-crowned Muses were born who worshipped dancing and singing. There were nine of them, as many as the nights of love it took to conceive them.

The Muses were not only the inspiration for artists and poets, being goddesses of the arts, dancing, dancing and music, but also guardians of the national cultural identity of the Greeks; key to better understanding the new course initiated by Zeus. Nature did not lose its power. Zeus remained the king of lightning and gales.

His brother Poseidon ruled the sea, disasters, earthquakes, and volcanoes. His sister Demeter was the goddess of fertility. Zeus married Hera, his sister; their marriage became a symbol of life and she herself a protector of family unions.

Even the place where Zeus chose to dwell was on earth: the summit of Mount Olympus, which was inhabited by relatives, sons and daughters, such as Athena, goddess of wisdom, and Hephaestus, God of craftsmanship.

Despite the defeat of the Titans, however, Zeus' rule remained fragile, and the battle for control of the 'universe would be a long one. The greatest challenge was posed by the huge bronze-covered monsters, children of the earth, who relentlessly sought to assault Olympus. Every time they were about to climb the mountains, which led to Olympus, they were pushed back down into the bowels of the earth.

According to well-established legend, the decisive clash took place in Italy in the Phlegrean fields near Naples, where the earth is said to still smoke given the violence of the fighting. Other traps were directed at Zeus by his hideous family. It is told in the Iliad that Zeus was forced to challenge his brothers and sisters one by one to establish himself as ruler of the gods and master of Olympus.

Prometheus, as he refused to submit to the Titans, refused to bow to the new king and hegemony of Zeus. From Prometheus' disobedience the whole human race benefited by receiving the discovery of fire as a gift. However, his torment was enormous, but more about that later.

Thanks to the myth of Pandora, mortal women entered the legend, and for Zeus, who was addicted to sex and mating (the approach compared to Cronus was totally different: Cronus devoured his children to remain the only one of his lineages, Zeus on the other hand mated with whomever he most pleased him, both mortals and gods, to keep his lineage going the longest) new territories of conquest opened up.

At that point, the story of Zeus was fueled by rapes, seductions, transformations and deceptions, resulting in a new generation of heroes, who constituted the junction between earth and heaven, the recognition of a vanished age when men and gods mingled with each other.

To satisfy his cravings, Zeus used the powers at his disposal by transforming himself whenever he wished into animals, rain, or men, which in turn attracted both gods and mortals. For example, to bewitch Leda, ruler of Sparta, he transformed himself into a beautiful swan. Their meeting generated two eggs: out of the first came Castor and Pollux, the Dioscuri. When the second opened, Helen, the most fascinating woman in the world, was born. To convince, however, the very young farmer Ganymede, Zeus transformed himself into an eagle. As the young man grazed his herds, Zeus flew above him, carrying him to Olympus, where he made Ganymede his drinking companion. To conquer Europa, a beautiful oriental girl, he transformed himself into a white-colored bull. Europa climbed onto the bull, taking her with him to Crete. Zeus resumed his appearance and several children were born of their union, including Minos, the future king of Crete. But his metamorphoses did not concern only the animal kingdom.

He once took on the features of the ruler of Thebes, Amphitryon, to take possession of his wife, Alcmene. To enjoy his conquest longer, he stopped the sun and extended the night by a few hours. From this union Herakles was born. The father of the deity also became enamored with Danae, daughter of the ruler Acrisius and Eurydice. The king was informed that his granddaughter would kill him, so he imprisoned his only daughter in a secret prison.

In order to get to the princess, Zeus turned into rain of gold. Perseus was the son of the love bond between Danae and Zeus.

Following the heroes of myth, the Macedonian ruler Alexander was the last one who could boast a divine lineage by making it a political tool. On the strength of this heritage, he pursued the conception of a world empire based on earthly life rather than life in heaven like his father Zeus. Alexander was unsuccessful in his pursuit, dying shortly thereafter in Babylon. His dominations would fragment to form several independent kingdoms. The Romans approached this concept of territorial vastness later, seeking to unify East and Africa to Europe.

In every city built, from Libya to Britain, from Syria to the Atlantic coast, a shrine was erected in the most important central square to Zeus, the one who had defeated the Chaos typical of the Titans' period of supremacy.

1.8 Age of men

The offspring of gold

The first humans, spawned by the gods, already existed in the time of Chronos. It was the Golden Age, and the world was ceaselessly cradled by a perpetual spring. The earth freely provided its crops, without the need to be brushed by the rake or torn by the plow. Zephyrs tended the flowers that sprang up without seed, the soils and crops were perpetually full of ears of corn, and rivers of milk and nutrients flowed over the earth.

As with the gods, the men of the royal lineage spent their lives with souls devoid of anguish, far removed from suffering and misery. They spent their days amid idleness and dancing. Without any kind of stress, they fed themselves on wild produce: all they had to do was reach out their hands to pluck the fruits of the haystack. Mountain strawberries, blackberries attached to thorny hedges, acorns falling from oak trees were just some of the delicacies they could pick without the slightest effort. They drank from the milk of goats and sheep, and fortified themselves with honey dripping from the plants.

Devoid of judges and laws, they honored righteousness and justice quite naturally. At that time there were no countries or walls, nor did men fight each other.

Everyone lived peacefully, in laziness, and did not he frequented other places than those in which he was born. There were no soldiers, no helmets, no armor, and no weapons of any kind.

And when the time came for them to die, they closed their eyes with the delicacy such as is typical of those who give themselves up to sleep. But with the deposition of Kronos, even this fortunate lineage was hidden underground. By order of the supreme Zeus, they became demons, earthly spirits, guardians of mortal men, and tireless spectators of their deeds, good or bad. Disguised by darkness, they went everywhere and were dispensers of riches and fortunes.

The progeny of silver

With the transition to the reign of Zeus, the Silver Age took over, certainly poorer than the Golden Age, but much richer and more privileged than the Bronze Age. Zeus gave the world four seasons: summer, inconstant autumn, cold winter, and a brief, timid spring. Thereafter, for the first time, the air became incandescent, parched by heat flushes; not all parts of the earth were hospitable and habitable as in the Golden Age.

A second progeny, much lower than the first, lived during this period. Some claim that it was created by the inhabitants of Olympus. According to others, however, they emerged from the bowels of the earth.

In the Silver Age, people-built shelters and dwellings for themselves for the very first time to protect themselves from the weather. Land was cultivated and oxen were used in plowing.

The silver lineage did not resemble the golden lineage at all, neither in appearance nor in spirit. Individuals of this era would remain as children for a hundred years, frolicking at home beside their venerable mothers. However, as soon as they crossed the threshold of youth and became men, their lives would last very little. Weakened and quarrelsome, they forgot to honor the immortal gods and make sacrifices in their honor. Zeus, therefore, outraged, hurled them underground. Transformed, they became the blessed of the underworld.

The offspring of bronze

Later the mighty Zeus begat another offspring of mortal men. The third, the bronze one, not at all similar to the silver offspring.
The bronze descendants were fearsome and aggressive, devoted solely to the conquests and bullying of Ares. Their equipment was made of bronze, their dwellings were made of bronze, and they themselves worked with bronze. They did not eat food made from grain, and they had hearts as hard as stones; were endowed with remarkable toughness, and had powerful bodies and mighty hands.
The bronze lineage consisted only of males. Created from the earth or dropped from trees, they did not require the presence of women to reproduce. The only women with whom they had experienced were nymphs. Zeus, to punish them, gave them Pandora, the first woman, the archetype of the female race, an instrument of incessant suffering for the entire male race.
The bronze men disappeared, killed with their own hands. Others say

Zeus destroyed them by causing a flood. The second bronze lineage, which preceded our own, was a race of demigods. The major protagonists of whom the legends tell were part of this lineage, including the famous Perseus, Heracles, Theseus, and Jason. They were defeated by treacherous battles: some under Thebes; others by ship, after the war had brought them to Troy because of a certain Helen.

Still others were subjugated by fate and died. Zeus placed them at the edge of the world, in the islands of the blessed, near the realm of Kronos.

The progeny of iron

The 'Bronze Age was followed by the Iron Age, our own. This was precisely the most squalid age; an age in which all men tormented themselves in labors and miseries, dragging their miserable existence amidst the pains that the deities inflicted on them.

Every imperfection intruded into men's lives. Frankness, demureness, and faithfulness disappeared. In their place came cheating, traps, overpowering, and the wretched pleasure of possession.

For the very first time, boundaries were delineated on earth's soil, at first common to all men just like light, sun and air. Men unfurled their sails to the wind, and cut down the groves of trees that had hitherto remained on the tops of lofty mountains.

They began to wander around going from earth to earth. They extracted from the bowels of the earth iron, previously unknown, gold, even more evil than iron. Both metals were the reason for increasingly bloody and bloody battles.

Human ferocity, reached its peak: children will outrage their relatives and not give them the necessities of life; husbands will plot the death of their wives, and wives that of their husbands; brothers will hardly come spared; stepmothers would become drunk with poisons; guests would no longer be sacred , and friends would lash out at each other.

The right of the strongest to prevail will be the only one in force in the Iron Age. Various wars will rage in cities already flooded with family blood.

Battles will rage and mansions will be looted.

Men will be cowardly, unscrupulous, ungrateful and bloodthirsty. The good and upright man will no longer have any respect, but all will do great honors to the bad and false. No covenant will be fulfilled anymore, and men will be united by the damnation of envy.

In fact, Aidos, the modest one, and Nemesis, the revengeful one, will leave the earth, returning to Mount Olympus, among the gods. Only Astraea, virgin deity of law, will oppose; but she too will depart. Men will be left with only sorrow and tears. There will no longer be any escape from evil.

Human life will be shorter and shorter, until children will be born already old, with white temples from birth. At this point, Zeus will also annihilate this human offspring.

Chapter 2
The Greek Heroes

2.1 Bellerophon

Bellerophon, the Hellenic hero who fell into ruin because of his pride. Bellerophon, was the great-grandson of Sisyphus, was born in Corinth and, as Homer claims, the gods gave him power, elegance and charm. He was very young when he was forced to leave his city; he had accidentally murdered a man. He therefore went to Tiryns, to the ruler Proetus, to be released from his crime. He stayed there for some time as their welcome guest. Princess Anteia became infatuated with the handsome young man but, having already been rejected by him, blamed him unjustly before her husband.

"Bellerophon abused me. You must kill him. If you don't, I will curse you!"

Proetus gave credence to his wife's words and became enraged . But he could not eliminate one of his guests, someone with whom he had enjoyed a meal in his home. He therefore had another idea. He called the boy back and told him:

"I have an assignment for you. I will take you on a nice trip. You will leave tomorrow in the morning."

That same night Bellerophon had a dream. Athena appeared to him, gave him a pair of reins and said:

"Tomorrow morning at dawn, go to the source of the Pyrenees. There you will find a winged steed, Pegasus, born of Medusa's head after Perseus cut it off. He had an impetuous temper, but I was able to tame him. He stands on Olympus and brings lightning to Zeus. He is the favorite of the Muses. The goddess disappeared and Bellerophon did as he was instructed. In the meantime, the ruler Proto had sent a missive to his wife's father, Iobates, ruler of Lycia, stating, "The young man who will deliver this letter to you has not respected you and your daughter. I beg you to remove him from the world of the living, kill him." He carefully sealed it with his seal and sent for Bellerophon, who had been prepared for departure.

"You will travel to Lycia, present yourself to the ruler Iobate and deliver this missive directly into his hands. Be sure to do everything I have told you with extreme care."

King Iobate graciously welcomed the boy and invited him to sit down to dinner with him. He asked him about his journey as he opened the letter. Later, when he did so, he was shocked at the idea of killing a guest. However, somehow he was obliged to satisfy his son-in-law. That boy had been quite aggressive with his granddaughter!

"Bellerophon, you must provide me with a most valuable service. You must eliminate the Chimera, daughter of Echidna, who frequently raids my territories."

Iobates was sure that the feat was unattainable. Bellerophon would never return.

The Chimera was told thus by Hesiod: unbeatable fire, tremendous and enormous, swift and vigorous. He possessed three heads: one of a fiery-looking lion, one of a goat and one of a serpent, like a mighty dragon. When Bellerophon spotted the Chimera, he rose into the air, mounting Pegasus, piercing her with his arrows. Next, he thrust a piece of iron into her jaws. The Chimera's fiery breath melted the lead, which descended down her throat until it burned her vital organs.

As soon as Iobates saw Bellerophon return, proud of the reckless feat he had just accomplished, he had to devise other ways to kill him.

First of all, he sent Bellerophon to fight against his opponents, the Solymians and Amazons. The great hero routed them all by turning in the air, sheltered from their arrows, and dropping great stones on their heads.

He then sent him to fight a brigade of pirates traveling in a boat whose prow was adorned with the figure of a lion and a serpent, led by a proud and impetuous warrior. Bellerophon repelled them all.

Returning victorious from all these exploits, Bellerophon was called by the ruler Iobates, who said to him:

"I realized that you are brave, daring, a true hero. I can no longer believe my son-in-law's statements. Read his missive."

Knowing the truth, the ruler pleaded for the boy's remission, gave him in marriage his daughter Philinoe, sister of Anteia, and designated him as heir to the throne of Lycia. Bellerophon had two sons, Hippolocus and Isander, and a daughter, Laodamia, who would give birth to the hero Sarpedon along with Zeus. When the old ruler died, he ascended the throne. But our hero's story did not end, for he had another 'venture during his old age.

Pegasus was still with him, and Bellerophon made a gesture of great pride to the gods. He climbed into the saddle of his faithful steed, rose into the air and headed for Olympus, intending to access it. Zeus did not allow this and sent a gnat that stung Pegasus under his tail, causing him to flinch. The hero, fell down, going back the way he came. The winged horse, however, arrived on Olympus and Zeus took him with him. It was his pack animal for carrying lightning. But not only that, Zeus placed Pegasus in the sky as a constellation.

Bellerophon fell into a bush and wandered the earth for a long time, crippled, blind, avoiding the roads traveled by men. The account of his death has not been bequeathed to us.

2.2 Heracles

A demigod, the product of the relationship between Zeus and Alcmena, Heracles was a heroic, sometimes funny, sometimes romantic man in whom strength, wit, boldness and sexual vigor prevailed.

As was mentioned earlier, Alcmena was the mother of Heracles. The real father was Zeus, while the earthly one was named Amphitryon, Alcmena's husband.

Zeus took the guise of Alcmena's groom, Amphitryon, pretending that he had recently returned from a battle that the man had gone on to win. The real groom returned home the same night and, in turn, conjoined with his wife, who then found herself conceiving, at the same time, two children by different fathers: Alcides, who would later be named Heracles, and Ificles.

It was clear from the start that Heracles was an unusual child. If Zeus was proud of him, the wife of the king of the gods, Hera, detested him. She would torment him for the duration of his existence. The goddess immediately began by sending two blue-scaled serpents to kill him. In front of them the doors opened and they silently slipped into little Heracles' room. Flames came out of their gaze and poison gushed from their jaws.

And while Alcmena cried out, Amphitryon watched smugly, young Heracles, who though he could not yet walk, he was able to smother the two snakes with absolute calmness and calmness. The seer Tiresias, summoned by Amphitryon after this feat, predicted that the little one would in the future rout numerous monsters.

Once, Zeus heard Heracles whining for lack of food. Zeus went to Thebes, grabbed the baby and took him to Olympus. Hera was resting, so Zeus placed the baby next to Hera's breast so that he could nurse it.

Some claim that, at that point, as soon as the goddess woke up and realized "who" was on her chest, she sneaked away in anger. According to others, however, the ravenous Heracles made a great feeding, failing to swallow all the milk.

Whatever happened, an abundant white jet came out of Hera's breast and ended up forming the Milky Way in the heavens. Heracles had the best teachers of his time and was trained in all practices.

The wise centaur Chiron trained him in hunting and especially in medicine - an art in which he was very skilled. His earthly father Amphitryon initiated him in chariot driving and chariot racing. Eurytus, who had a huge bow given to him by his grandfather Apollo, explained to him how to shoot with this weapon, which remained forever, along with the mace, the hero's favorite.

Even one of the Dioscuri, Castor, gave him some fencing lessons. The famous Linus was also his teacher. The latter was the son of a muse and tried to impart to him the art of reading words and playing melodies. However, Heracles was not at all inclined in these disciplines and was a poor and apathetic student.

One afternoon Linus, in exasperation, scolded him:

"You are lazy. You don't care what I teach you and you learn absolutely nothing!"

Linus beat him with a riding crop. To protect himself, Heracles took the lyre and hurled it at the back of the teacher's head. Because of the strength of his arm, the blow was terrible and Linus died.

Heracles was not chastised since he had reacted in self- defense, but Amphitryon was not satisfied: the young man had become too strong. He stopped Heracles' studies and sent him out to graze cattle until he was eighteen years old.

Thereafter, Heracles began to wander the world, attempting to do good for humankind.

This prompted him to perform his first feats, such as clashing with the bandit Termerus, who loved to murder wayfarers by subjecting them to a duel with his head. One day this bandit challenged Heracles and to his great disappointment he discovered that the demigod's skull was so much harder than his own that it shattered in the blink of an eye.

After beating a lion on the mountain Cytaeron, and being a guest of the ruler Thespius for a short time, our hero had fifty children with the daughters of the ruler, who, yearning to have the same offspring as him, went to him every night, leading him to believe that he was always the same person.

Only one, who wanted to remain unmarried, refused. The others joined him, bearing children incessantly; one of them even had twins. Later he returned to Thebes and met the heralds of the ruler of Orchomenus, who arrived there to demand war tribute. Infuriated by their attitude, the hero rebelled and cut off their noses and ears, then sent them back to their ruler, thus provoking an assault due to revenge.

In the ensuing battle, Heracles made a great show of himself and killed, with his own hands, the ruler of Orchomenus. The battle was not without losses, however; Amphitryon was in fact one of those casualties.

At the end of the battle against Orchomenus, Heracles obtained as a prize the hand of Megara, eldest daughter of Creon, the ruler of Thebes. The two lived together for some time in Amphitryon's court.

However, during a time when the hero was away, Megara was raped by Lycus. As soon as Heracles learned of this, he eliminated Lycus in a very violent way. But Hera, his great enemy, drove him mad and he, in an excess of fury, took the three children and killed them, throwing them into the fire.

He intended to continue with the slaughter, eliminating Megara as well, but Athena, his protector, intervened and hurled a large rock at his chest. Heracles collapsed into a deep sleep.

Upon his awakening, the hero immediately regained rationality. What he had committed returned to his memory. Desperate, he locked himself for three days in a dark room.

" What can I do to obtain forgiveness for the tremendous crime I committed?" This was the question that nagged at him incessantly.

So he decided to travel to Delphi, where the Pythia, Apollo's priestess, spoke on behalf of the god.

The Pythia sat on a golden wooden tripod, gnawing on laurel leaves. First, she had Heracles intervene. He told her his dramatic story. Then she pronounced herself as follows:

"You, Alcides (up to that time that was his name), are to go to Tiryns together with your cousin Eurystheus.

For years you will have to serve and do whatever he orders you to do. This will be done in the name of Hera. So, starting now, you will be called Heracles, which means "glory of Hera." These will be very hard years for you, but they will guarantee you fame in the millennia and enable you to ascend Olympus upon your death and acquire immortality."

Heracles did not intend to place himself in the service of Eurystheus, a man who was inferior to him for many years, but such was the choice of the gods and he was obliged to listen to it.

Eurystheus informed him that, to set him free, he would subject him to ten labors.

At the end of the first ten trials, however, two more were added, as Eurystheus refused to accept two of them as accomplished. One was the defeat of the Hydra of Lerna, since, in order to beat her, Heracles was joined by his nephew Iolaus, son of Iphiclus. The second was the cleaning of Augea's stables, as the hero had accepted, though not received, a payment.

The deities gave him these gifts:

Hermes: a splendid sword
Apollo: a bow and arrows adorned with eagle feathers Hephaestus: a golden breastplate
Athena: a coat Poseidon: two horses.
Zeus: a marvelous shield. Such a shield, the work of Hephaestus, had a band around it imprinted with the heads of twelve serpents. At each of Heracles' battles, the serpents' heads opened their jaws, intimidating their opponents.
In the following chapter, we will find out about his twelve labors.

When Heracles went toward the first of the labors, he crossed Egypt and experienced another adventure.
Busiris reigned there. He was the son of Poseidon and was a very evil ruler. He had forced the sea deity Proteus to flee and had tried to kidnap the Hesperides, the Sunset Nymphs, famous for their loveliness. He was such a despot that a famine struck Egypt.
Busiris therefore questioned a certain fortune teller who came from Cyprus, and received this response:

"To end hunger, it is necessary to sacrifice a stranger to Zeus every year."
Busiris immediately began to have as many foreigners as possible sacrificed.

The next year Heracles arrived and the unwary ruler took him and bound him. Afterwards Busiris adorned him with flowers and led him toward the altar for sacrifice. Heracles, who had waited patiently for such a moment, broke the laces, fell to the ground and killed Busiris, thus saving Egypt from such an evil ruler. There were numerous other expeditions of Heracles that were not strictly related to the Twelve Labors, although some of them were carried out in past years in the service of Eurystheus.

In addition to taking part in the Argonauts' expedition along with Jason, at least until the Boreans persuaded their leader to leave him behind, Heracles eliminated countless giants, including Cycnus, Porphyry (who, thus, was precluded from raping Hera), and Antheus, immortal until in contact with the earth, who was murdered as the hero lifted him off the ground by strangling him.

Among his many secondary exploits, Heracles faced Dionysus in a drinking contest, even defeating death itself by physically preventing it from snatching the life from Alcestis, wife of Admetus, ruler of Pherae and argonaut.

Having completed the twelve labors, Heracles returned to Thebes, his great city. More or less ten years had passed since his departure. His grandson, Iolaus, had now become a man and a powerful athlete who had achieved victory in the chariot race at the Olympics. Recall that Iolaus, who was still a boy, had been the driver of Heracles' charioteer when they went to Lerna to defeat the Hydra.

Acheloos was the largest stream in Greece and flowed from Epirus to the Ionian Sea. He was the first of the 3,000 children created by Oceanus and Tethis when the world was created. He was the father of sirens and many other sea creatures. As the god of rivers, Acheloos had the power to transform himself into whatever he wanted.

He always wished to be honored and was furious with those who did not. So one day, at a festival honoring the gods, there were a small group of Naiads, the nymphs of the springs, who had honored all the gods except him. And what did Acheloo do? These are his words in the verses of the poet and writer Ovid:

"...with great force and an immense flood, I uprooted the trees from the forests, the meadows from the fields, and finally the nymphs who will finally remember me..."

Then he carried them out to sea by his current, trapped them and turned them into rock. Thus the Echinads islands were born.

The town of Calydon was located at the mouth of that river, and Acheloos had the opportunity to observe and appreciate the beautiful Deianira several times. He had fallen in love with her and asked for her hand in marriage.

But the girl refused to marry him as she was frightened by the idea that he might turn into some hideous beast at will.

On the contrary, Heracles proposed to the girl to marry him, and she accepted instantly. This infuriated Acheloos, who challenged him. Before and during the challenge, there was an exchange of strong accusations between the two. Heracles began, bragging about what he could give the girl:

"If Deianira marries me, she will have Zeus as her father-in- law and a groom famous for his deeds!"

Acheloo, in the guise of a bull with the head of a man, smiled and affirmed:

"I am the founder of every Greek river and not an outsider like you! Near Dodona there is an oracle of Zeus, and it demands that I make a sacrifice before receiving the response!"

In saying this, because the challenge had already begun, Acheloo found himself lying on the ground, with Heracles on top of him. He then mutated into a grass snake and crawled away. Heracles affirmed:

"I am not afraid of you. I choked snakes when I was still an infant in a cradle." And he laughed.

Heracles began to grab the snake by the neck, but all of a sudden he was confronted by a bull, which attacked him.

Heracles cleverly dodged the bull and grabbed it by the horns.

He hurled the bull to the ground with such force that the right horn shattered remaining in his hands.

At one point, Acheloos, embarrassed, abandoned the challenge, giving up the beautiful princess. It is said that he retrieved his horn by offering Heracles, the horn of prosperity, the Cornucopia.

Heracles, therefore, married Deianira. The couple lived for several periods in Calydon where a child was born: Hyllus.

Afterwards, the newlyweds left the city, and on the way they had to cross a river. There was no bridge, but a boatman. This was the centaur Nessus, who offered to carry Deianira, while Heracles would swim to the other bank.

The centaur bowed at the woman's feet, and she climbed onto his back with complete ease.

In carrying the woman, Nessus tried to grasp her violently, but she struggled to defend herself, screaming aloud. Enraged, Heracles eliminated Nexus.

Some say he used one of his poisonous arrows; others say he used a sword. But a third myth states that Heracles struck Nessus with his own hands.

The supreme Heracles certainly could not have foreseen the repercussions of his act. At the point of death, the centaur turns to Deianira and says:

"I'll tell you a secret. Take some of my blood: It is a kind of enchanted filter. Should Heracles leave you for another woman in the future, moisten his tunic with the said filter and he will immediately return to you."

Nessus expired, and in the process Deianira placed a few drops of his blood in a vial, hiding it very carefully.

The newlyweds then settled in Trachis, in the vicinity of the ruler Ceyx. But the indefatigable hero was unable to sit still and resumed wandering. In solitude, he headed for Oechalia.

In Oechalia, Eurytus reigned. He had two sons, Iphitus and Iole. Iole was very attractive and had many suitors. Her father, a particularly skilled archer, claimed that he would allow his daughter to marry only the one who defeated him in an archery challenge. Heracles, who had meanwhile learned the use of this weapon from Eurytus, presented himself and won it. But the ruler knew that Heracles, several years earlier, in a moment of madness, had murdered his sons. Out of fear that, in the future, the hero might have done the same thing to Iole's children, he refused to celebrate their marriage.

Heracles' wrath was devastating. He hurled young Iphitus off the walls. Moreover, Iphitus had been the only one to protect him and was absolutely innocent.

This was a very terrible crime, for which Heracles had to purify himself. To find out how, Heracles went to Delphi. But the Pythia would not answer him. Heracles, probably not fully recovered from the madness, began to rant threateningly:

"I will raze the temple, take the treasures, deruberate the tripod on which the Pythia sits, and establish a new oracle elsewhere!"

How could Pythia, who was old and frail, counter Heracles? He therefore invoked Apollo, who rushed in favor of his own priestess. Thus a fight broke out between the two, both brothers, both sons of Zeus. The father hurled a thunderbolt and separated them. Heracles gave up the fight. Finally, the Pythia gave her verdict:

"You will be surrendered as a slave and serve for three long years.

Now we return to Lydia, where a beautiful young ruler named Omphale ruled. One day, Omphale purchased a slave. He was a strong, sturdy man who wore a lion's fur while holding a club.

The queen commissioned him with several challenges, some very difficult and risky, which the man always managed to overcome with great facility.

She appreciated his talent and recognizing him as the famous hero fell in love with him.

The story goes that Heracles loved the queen so much that he put his lion skin on her, amusing her with the club, while he learned how to spin wool, wearing her purple robes. Whenever he made some mistake in spinning, she would playfully beat him by hitting him with her golden sandal! Three years passed quickly and Heracles' imprisonment ended so that he could return to Oechalia.

Our protagonist had not forgotten that Iole had been denied to him. He had won her in the archery challenge against Eurytus, the girl's father, who subsequently broke his word. His ego and anger were very intense, moreover, Iole was very attractive and Heracles wanted her all to himself.

Thanks to his army, Heracles was in the process of destroying the city. Iole-perhaps the only one in all the legends we know-did not like the hero. In order not to fall into his clutches, she threw herself down from a high turret. However, her wide robes allowed her to gently plummet to the ground while avoiding injury. Heracles abducted her and treated her as if she were his bride, disregarding Deianira, who was far away.

Deianira remained alone in her own abode. For years her husband had been away, and news had spread that he had fallen in love with a certain Iole. She remembered Nessus' filter and waited for the right moment to win him back (she still believed in their love).

So, one day young Lichas, Heracles' messenger, came and asked her:
"Your husband wants a different tunic, a new tunic since he is to dedicate an altar to Zeus in recognition of a victory of his own."

Deianira sprinkled the tunic with the blood of Nessus and gave it to Lyca.

When Heracles dressed her, he felt an awesome heat in all his joints that drove him mad with pain. He took the young Lichas and hurled him far away, in the direction of the sea, where he was transformed into the Lichadi Islands.

At the same time, the silk dress became more and more stuck, and could no longer separate from the body.

Thus, as soon as the hapless Deianira realized what Heracles had done, she committed suicide.

Heracles went to Mount Oeta. There was no one there. He extirpated much of the forest and made a pyre in which he settled. He had with him his famous bow and poison-tipped arrows. Just then, a very young boy appeared. His name was Philoctetes.

"Burn the pyre," Heracles told him, "And I will give you all my weapons. But promise me that you will not reveal to a living soul in what place this happened."

So it happened, and the giant pyre began to burn.

A prediction of Zeus came true: "No mortal can ever eliminate Heracles, but an already deceased enemy will sanction his demise." No sooner had the first flames risen on the pyre than lightning crashed down from the sky, turning everything to dust.

Athena, the goddess who had always protected Heracles, descended on a cloud. She led a chariot with four steeds. The hero climbed into it, and she accompanied him to Olympus. At the same time, there was a council among the gods, at which Hera agreed to accept Heracles as her own son, since he had earned this good fortune through his endeavors, his courage, and, especially, his pains.

Athena led the hero before the throne of Zeus, who proclaimed him as an immortal being.

Zeus and Hera had a child, Hebe, the goddess of youth and cupbearer of the gods. This became Hera's consort.

But now he was a deity, and each god had an assignment: there was the god of battle, the god of the sea, the goddess of wisdom, and so on. Heracles therefore became the guardian of the heavens, never tiring of guarding the gates of Olympus.

Among the shadows of the dead who wandered in Erebus, there was also a faint shadow of Heracles, to remind him that he had been the son of a mortal woman. Later he would meet Odysseus, but that is another story....

2.3   Perseus

"Perseus, son of Zeus, slayer of Medusa, protector of Andromeda."

Perseus belonged to a lineage that was half royal and half divine.

His grandfather, Acrisius, ruler of Argos, had married Eurydice and had a daughter, Danae, but unfortunately he had no male successor to whom he could cede his kingdom. This caused him to turn to the Oracle of Delphi, who, instead of answering him, gave him unwanted information: Acrisius was destined to succumb because of his daughter's offspring.

At the time, Danae was unmarried. To make sure she remained so, her father imprisoned her in an open-air bronze prison in the garden of the royal palace, manned by ferocious dogs to block anyone who might approach and attack the young girl's purity.

In this way, he presumably achieved the very thing he wanted to avoid. However, the maiden was spotted by Zeus himself, who, as was well known, certainly did not flinch if it came to ensnaring a beautiful woman. So, Zeus mutated into a golden rain, sneaked into the cage and joined Danae, who thus gave birth to Perseus.

Acrisius was thus faced with quite a dilemma: to risk his own life or to outrage the king of the gods by having his son killed?

Faced with the dilemma, he did what any sensible person would have accomplished-or perhaps not. He eliminated the nursemaid, locked Danae and Perseus in a chest and threw them into the sea, which meant in a sense abandoning them to the mercy of the gods.

And, in fact, they turned out to be compassionate.

The chest ran aground on the shores of the island of Serifos, where it was found by a sailor, Dictys, brother of the island's ruler, Polydektes. The latter immediately thought it contained a treasure of great value.

The fisherman rescued the two castaways and raised Perseus as his own son. In the process, he became infatuated with Danae and developed an attraction for her. In this, his brother was quite similar to him, and he tried in various circumstances to win the girl, but she rejected him and Perseus himself resisted.

To get rid of the young man's encroachments, Polidektes claimed he wanted to take Queen Hippodamia as his wife for political reasons and asked each guest for a horse as a wedding gift.

Perseus was unable to give anything as a gift, but he certainly could not lose the chance to make his mother free of the unseemly suitor. Thus, he promised Polidektes that he would give him whatever gift he wished as long as it left Danae alone for good.

Without adding more, the ruler demanded the head of Medusa, the only one among the Gorgons who was mortal. She possessed snakes for hair and was capable of turning anyone who crossed her gaze into rock. Polydektes claimed that Perseus would not succeed in the feat and would not return to thwart him.

But the deities had other plans for the young demigod.

To support his son in this endeavor, Zeus gave him a very sharp diamond sword and allowed him to use the helmet of Hades, which could make those who used it completely invisible.

Hermes gave him his winged boots as a gift. Athena gave him a shield as shiny as a mirror and warned him that in order to succeed in carrying Medusa's head, whose power would not fade upon her death, it required a sack guarded by the Hesperides, the nymphs in charge of protecting Hera's garden, the exact location of which was unknown to most.

In order to find the latter, Perseus was forced to ask the Graeae or Phorcides, sisters of the Gorgons. These were three women, perpetually old, blind, and without more teeth. The three women had only one eye and one tooth, which they therefore had to use in turn.

To force them to assist him, Perseus took away their one eye at the handover, returning it only after being led to the garden of the Hesperides.

So, equipped and armed, Perseus set out in search of Medusa, passing through a forest of sculptures that were petrified men, finding her sleeping with her sisters in their cave.

Making himself invisible and proceeding backwards, so that he was not looking directly at her but only from the reflection of his shield, the protagonist approached Medusa and cut off her head with the sword Zeus had given him.

From the severed throat of the Gorgon emerged a steed with wings, Pegasus, and a colossus, Chrysaurus, children of the earlier story between her and Poseidon, god of the seas.

The other Gorgons chased after Perseus, but to no avail. They were unable to spot him because of the helmet of
 Hades and could not chase after him because of Hermes' sandals, which allowed him to take flight.

On the way back, Perseus had other minor exploits. Among them was his acquaintance with Atlas, who was forced to bear the weight of the world on his shoulders and who, out of pity, turned him into stone to take him out of his drudgery.

Atlas was wary of foreigners because of a prophecy that his kingdom would be annihilated by one of Zeus' sons. Unfortunately, Perseus (who did not know about the prophecy) revealed his celestial origin. Learning of this, Atlas tried to kill him. The young man, astonished by his reaction, was forced to have to defend himself in an unequal battle against the titan until, having opened the saddlebag where he kept Medusa's head, he put an end to the duel. Atlas began to petrify, turning into a tall mountain.

Perseus then flew over Ethiopia and stayed there to admire a beautiful maiden tied to a rock. This was Andromeda, daughter of the ruler Cepheus and his vain Cassiopeia. The latter dared to claim that her daughter was just as beautiful as the Nereids, the nymphs of the seas, thus arousing the wrath of Poseidon, who induced him to bombard the kingdom with tidal waves and unleash a great sea monster, Cetus, against it. The premise for the god end her sentence was for Andromeda to be immolated to the giant being - Perseus met her in this situation.

To appease Poseidon's anger, Andromeda was condemned to sacrifice. Perseus proposed to save her in exchange for the ruler's promise to marry her.

Perseus won the challenge easily but, at the time of the wedding, he had to face a small group of armored men led by Phineas, Andromeda's uncle, to whom her hand had been promised. Perseus resolved the situation by unsheathing the head of Medusa, which he always kept with him, and reduced all the assailants to stone. He subsequently ran away with Andromeda, holding her hand.

Perseus returned with his new wife to Seriphos, to the dismay of Polydektes, who, in his absence, had accentuated his ruthless courtship of Danae by trying to force her to marry him. On that occasion, Perseus made use of Medusa's head for the last time, turning Polydektes into stone and putting Danae and her now companion Dictys on the throne. Then Perseus returned the tools that had been lent to him by the deities and gave Athena the severed head, which she used to adorn Zeus' shield.

That done, Perseus chose to return to Argos, unaware of why he was initially exiled. It was not his will to fulfill the Oracle's prophecy; nevertheless, he ended up doing so quite inadvertently. Although there are discordant versions of this myth, in each of them Acrisius always remains a victim of Perseus merely because he happened to be in the path of his throw in the course of a sports competition.

Following the burial of his grandfather outside the city of Larissa, Perseus obtained the kingdom of Argos as an inheritance, but he did not want to rule.

Thus, he proposed to Megapenthes, successor of Proetus, an exchange of realm. So he established Mycenae and had seven sons (Perses, Heleus, Alcaeus, Mestor, Electryon, Sthenelus and Cynurus) and two daughters (Gorgophone and Autochthe). This was a lineage that would later lead to the birth of Heracles (Amphitryon was the son of Alcaeus, and, as we mentioned earlier his wife Alcmena bore the son of Zeus, Heracles). After Perseus's death, the goddess Athena, to celebrate his fame, turned him into a constellation, which she placed near her beloved Andromeda and her mother Cassiopeia, whose velleity had driven the two to cross paths. Even today, observing the sky, one can see the three constellations in remembrance of their existences and, mainly, of the strong love between the two boys.

2.4 Theseus

Theseus, the Hellenic hero of semi-divine extraction who defeated the Minotaur and unified Attica with Athens.

Theseus was a legendary hero, famous primarily for his duel against the terrifying Minotaur. This hero is credited with the political reunification of Attica under Athens.

Like many other heroes of his generation, Theseus boasted semi-divine origins and, in addition to his mother Ahetra, was the son of two fathers, Aegeus and Poseidon, the god of the seas.

Aegeus, desiring a descendant and having no clear ideas on the matter, headed to the Oracle of Delphi to find out how to have a son. The oracle gave him a solution to the problem that Aegeus did not understand. Thereafter, he relied on the wise ruler Pittheus of Troezen.

The latter, instead of answering his question, handed over his daughter, Aethra.

On her wedding night, Aethra found herself wandering the coast and crossing the sea to the island of Sphairia, where she was lured by Poseidon. The end result of which was the conception of a little one who had a mixture of earthly and divine characteristics.

When Aethra found herself pregnant, Aegeus considered returning to Athens. But before he left, he buried his shoes and his saber under a boulder, stating that once his son grew up, he should prove his right to the title by removing the boulder and finding the objects. He then left Ahetra and, returning home, married Medea, who had been hiding there after she killed Jason's sons out of spite. Jason had then left her for another woman.

This cycle of abandonment was probably an inspiration to Theseus, who never missed an opportunity to abandon the various women who came his way.

Theseus was born in his mother's lands, unaware of who his father was, until he was sixteen years old, when he became strong enough to be able to move the boulder and take back the shoes and saber that had been left there especially for him. Then Etra revealed the truth to him and suggested that he take the objects back to his father and claim his right of primogeniture.

Theseus could travel as far as Athens by sea, a quick and danger-free journey, or by land, which would take him along the Saronic Gulf and past six entrances to the afterlife, each guarded by a powerful guardian. Needless to say, he opted for the latter.

The first duel took place in the very city of Epidaurus, dedicated to Apollo, where the brigand Periphetes, son of Hephaestus, killed travelers by beating them with his bronze club with such power that he hurled them to the ground. Theseus eliminated him by throwing a huge boulder at him or, according to other versions, by stealing his club and using it to strike him. Later he began to use only the club, which he decided to carry with him at all times.

Having reached the entrance to the Isthmus of Corinth, Theseus fought against Sinis, who used to seize his victims by tying their feet to two different pine trees that he had arranged to bend on the ground. He would then let go of the trees thus quartering the unfortunate victim. Theseus, once battered and having given him the same treatment, lay with his daughter. From their union came Perigune and Melanippus.

Not far from the isthmus, Theseus eliminated the gigantic Crommian sow, which, according to various accounts, was created by an old shrew called Phaea, most likely one of the many beings procreated by Typhon and Echidna.

Near Megara, Theseus crossed paths with the bandit Sciron, who forced wayfarers to cross a narrow coastal path in order to wash their feet. Later, while they were bent over, he threw them off a cliff so that they could be devoured by a sea monster, or probably a giant turtle.

The hero made him meet the same end that he reserved for his poor, unwitting victims.

In the historic city of Eleusis, Theseus won a duel against the ruler Cercyon. According to some accounts, the ruler used to challenge wayfarers by killing them after defeating them, instead, according to others, he was a dedicated sacrificial ruler who, every year-end, had to fight for his life against some challenger. The winner became ruler only after eliminating the challenger. Theseus killed Cercion after he defeated him, but he did not want to take his place.

Finally, on the plain of Eleusis, the protagonist dueled against the bandit Procrustes. He had two beds of different sizes and made one of them available to travelers passing through. If they were unfit for the size of the bed, he would remedy the situation by stretching their limbs or severing the excess parts. Again, Theseus killed the highwayman by paying him with his own coin.

Arriving in Athens, Theseus did not immediately reveal his identity to his father. Aegeus received him at his court, although he was suspicious of his intentions. But Medea quickly realized who he was and worried that he might ascend the throne in place of Medo, her only son with Aegeus. To prevent this, she proposed that Theseus kill the bull of Marathon.

It was a powerful bovine that blew fire from its nostrils, formerly known as the bull of Crete, and with which Pasiphae, wife of the king of Crete, Minos, brother of Aegeus, had given rise to the Minotaur. The bull, after being captured by Heracles in his seventh effort, was freed and taken to Marathon.

On the way, Theseus took refuge, in the midst of a storm, in the hut of the old woman Ecale, who promised to make a sacrifice in honor of Zeus if he succeeded in capturing the bull. Unfortunately, by the time the hero returned with the animal, the old woman was already deceased. Therefore, Theseus thought of naming one of the regions of Attica after her.

Having returned to Athens with the bull and having sacrificed it, Theseus ran the risk of being killed with poison at the hands of Medea. He was rescued in extremis by Aegeus, who, at last recognized him by his sandals and sword, snatching, therefore, from his hands the poisoned chalice of wine.

Medea, was discovered, and fled to Asia. Arriving in Athens, Theseus conducted other exploits, probably also contributing to the journey with the Argonauts. Certainly, he was in the presence of Heracles on the day the latter went to the lands of the Amazons for the ninth of his labors; namely, that of recovering the belt of Princess Hippolyta.

In this place, Theseus fell in love with the princess Hippolyta, or perhaps her sister Antiope, and captured her to be his bride. From her he had a son, Hippolytus.

The sports games were held in Athens once every five years, and paladins from different kingdoms took part. Among them was Androgeus, the eldest son of the ruler of Crete, Minos, who had distinguished himself by achieving excellent results in every test and winning several. This was not at all accepted by the Pallantids, the grandsons of Aegeus, who decreed to settle the matter in the most immediate way possible: by eliminating their rival.

When the news reached him, Minos sailed his fleet toward Athens, declaring war on the city. It is not entirely clear whether Aegeus won or regretted the incident.

In any case, even the ruler of Athens was unaware of who had carried out this murder. Therefore, he offered a sacrifice of human lives in return: once every seven years, the seven most valiant young men and seven most attractive virgins of Athens would be offered in sacrifice to Crete.

None of them would ever return, as Minos ordered that they be fed to the Minotaur, the fruit of the zoophilic relationship between his wife Pasiphae and the Cretan bull, the

Which lived in the labyrinth created by Daedalus. Let us review some of the history.

Poseidon gave Minos a magnificent white bull with very long horns. Queen Pasiphae, when she saw it, fell in love with it to the point that she wanted to marry it. Then she asked Daedalus, a famous inventor and builder, to give her advice. Daedalus was an Athenian, but he had to leave his city, moving with his son to Knossos. He was able not only to construct buildings and monuments, but also to build machinery and solve a variety of problems.

The queen, therefore, turned to him. Daedalus built her a white wooden heifer, empty inside, in which the queen could access and hide. In this way she was able to stay close to the bull and cheat it as if it were a real cow. Thus was born Asterion, the Minotaur, a hideous monster who possessed the physique of a man, completely covered with hair, and a head like that of a bull.

Minos thought to keep this horrendous incident hidden. He ordered Daedalus to create a suitable place to lock up the monster.

Daedalus began work and created a vast, immense palace (some say underground) consisting of such a mixture of halls, rooms, lanes, and intersections that it was practically impossible, for all those who had entered it, to identify a way out.

It was in this very labyrinth that the Minotaur was imprisoned. As he grew up, he began to become aggressive and feed on human flesh.

Once the Labyrinth was finished, Minos decided that Daedalus should be locked up with his son Icarus. This was for two reasons: first, it was a punishment for the engineer who had made the wooden heifer, and second, to prevent anyone from discovering what was hidden in it.

Daedalus was not discouraged. He immediately took action to get out of there. Using bird feathers glued with wax, he made large wings that he fastened on his son's shoulders and his own.

Before then no one had ever succeeded in flying. Their attempt was extremely dangerous; Daedalus turned to Icarus, with tears in his eyes recommending:

" Listen, my son. Once you leave, stay close to me. Under no circumstances should you fly at too high an altitude, otherwise the sun will melt the wax. Do not fly excessively low as the feathers will risk being dampened by the sea. I repeat, stay close and do not change your direction. You will see that everything will be all right."

They began to beat their wings, moved and emerged from an opening in the wall.

They rose into the air and, as they flew away from the island toward the northeast, flapping their wings repeatedly, the villagers, sailors and peasants who turned their gaze to the sky and saw them, mistook them for gods.

At first, father and son were reluctant, but then they took courage. Even too much: the careless boy did not listen to his father and, elated by the flight, reached higher and higher. The wax dissolved and Icarus plunged into the sea.

It is said that Daedalus was able to escape from the island and fly to Italy. He landed in Cumae, after which he settled in Sicily, where he continued his business by building numerous palaces.

On the third such expedition, Theseus volunteered to join the sacrificed youth (and to kill the monster). Some claim that he killed it with a spear, others with a club, and still others with his bare hands. Theseus, therefore, joined the victims incognito and sailed out to sea on a ship with wide black sails, swearing to his father Aegeus that if he was able to complete the feat, he would raise white sails on his return to proclaim his victory even before he reached the shore.

Actually, the boy set out armed only with confidence and a lot of good will, as his weapons were confiscated from him, as they were from all the other boys sent to die in Crete. His mission would have ended with ease had it not been for a rather joyful little maiden, Ariadne, the daughter of Minos, who fell in love with the young man from the first glance, offering to help him eliminate the Minotaur (who, let us not forget, was even his brother on his mother's side) o n one condition: on his return to Athens he would have to take her away with him.

The night before the sacrifice, the maiden led Theseus to the gates of the labyrinth and gave him a poisoned sword and a ball of thread to untie on the way, so that on his return he would be able to find his way out easily. She also told him the directions that the creator of the labyrinth, Daedalus, had given her. This would enable Theseus to reach the center of the structure, where the Minotaur dwelt.

The suggestion given by Daedalus in fact must not have been exactly trustworthy, since he had never been able to get out of the labyrinth in question except as a result of creating wax wings so that he could escape by flying. In any case, Theseus managed to make his way to the heart of the palace and, after a fierce struggle, managed to bring down the Minotaur.

Once the beast was decapitated, the boy retraced the path traced by Ariadne's thread, emerged unharmed, and escaped along with the Athenian children who had left with him.

And as promised, he also managed to take with him Ariadne and her younger sister Phaedra (his intention was to leave the former on the island of Naxos and marry the latter, his sister).

The return to Athens was not as planned. Perhaps because of forgetfulness, perhaps because of a curse cast by Ariadne, perhaps because of the destruction of the white sails, or perhaps because, in spite of everything, Theseus had grown tired of his father, the ship arrived in port with the black sails set. Seeing them, and convinced that his son was dead, Aegeus killed himself by jumping into the sea that today bears his very name.

Theseus was elected ruler and first gathered all the men and women of Athens, scattered across the countryside, into one great city.

The second thing Theseus did after ascending the throne was to disown his wife, Hippolyta, or Antiope, since she had decided to marry Phaedra. The Amazon returned to her homeland only to reappear on her wedding day in the presence of an army of soldiers, announcing that anyone who took part in the celebrations would be killed.

However, the woman found death during the clashes that followed.

Theseus was, therefore, able to marry Phaedra without further hindrance, and he had two sons with her, Demophon and Acamas.

After a short time, however, Phaedra fell in love with Hippolytus, who rejected her outright but not because she had been the cause of her mother's death, but rather to preserve a vow of chastity taken before Artemis.

According to some rumors, it was Aphrodite who made the woman fall in love with him, as punishment for choosing the cult of Artemis over her own (although it is unclear how the love of a beautiful woman could be a punishment). Angered by such an outrage, Phaedra ran to Theseus, claiming that Hippolytus had raped her. In any case, after her husband killed Hippolytus to chastise him for a crime he had never done, the woman took her own life out of a sense of remorse.

The ruler of the Lapiths, Pyritus, himself a son of the father of the gods Zeus, had heard of Theseus' bravery and exploits and had therefore decided to test him by stealing his cattle herds. When Theseus set out in pursuit and found him, the two clashed but were so impressed with each other that they stopped the fight and made an oath of friendship that would last for years to come.

Together, the two tried their hand at several exploits, including hunting the wild boar Calydonius, probably the son of the sow of Crommyonia, already prey to Theseus at the time of his passage to Athens.

Theseus was also invited to Pyrito's wedding banquet with Hippodamia, which was attended even by centaurs. As per tradition, the centaurs got drunk and tried to steal the bride. However, the Lapiths and Theseus beat them, leading them back to their lands. On that occasion, Theseus beat Eurytus, "the most violent of all the violent centaurs."

Later, the two friends decided that since they both had divine ancestry, they should marry the daughters of Zeus. Theseus opted for Helen of

Troy, while Pyrrhus preferred Persephone, a former bride of Hades.

So the pair descended into the underworld to perform a second abduction. However, as they walked through those dark places, the two decided to stop for a moment and relax on top of a rock. Soon they found that they could no longer get up. Surrounded by the Furies, they faced an eternity of torment.

Theseus would later be rescued by Heracles, who had descended to the underworld for his twelfth and final effort. But for Pyrrhus there was nothing to be done.

Returning from the dead, Theseus later realized that the Dioscuri had freed Helen, taking her to Sparta, and installed Menestheus on the throne of Athens.

While Theseus' life was glorious and eventful, this was not the case with his death. He was thrown from a cliff by the ruler of Scyros, Lycomedes, aided by Menestheus.

And what about Arianna?

Upon her awakening, Ariadne found herself to be alone. Anxious at first, then desperate, she set out to find Theseus. But he was nowhere to be seen, and when she turned her gaze to the sea, she noticed a distant sail disappearing over the horizon.

She began to cry, but her sobs soon ceased as she heard cheerful sounds and singing approaching.

It was the procession of Dionysus: the god on his chariot drawn by cats, surrounded by Maenads and Satyrs, and escorted by the inseparable old man Silenus.

He was captivated by the beautiful princess and immediately asked her to become his bride, giving her a precious gift: a chiseled gold tiara, which is now in the sky in the form of a constellation, the Corona Borealis.

Ariadne agreed to the proposal and to Dionysus' gift; she went with him to Olympus, thus becoming immortal.

2.5   Jason

Jason, the Hellenic hero, captain of a cursed ship in search of the Golden Fleece.

This legend begins with an abuse of power. After the demise of the Cretan ruler, over the throne of Iolco was to sit Heson the legitimate son the ruler had by his wife Tyre. However, the ruler's wife also conjoined Poseidon, with whom she had two sons. One of these, Pelias-though already at a very advanced age-removed Aeson from the throne and killed all his relatives for fear of being ousted, but spared him out of love for his mother, Tyre. Pelias had him imprisoned in the palace, guarded day and night, but this did not preclude Aeson from uniting with his wife, Alcymede, who would give birth to a son, Diomedes. This boy was destined for certain death; therefore, his mother declared that she had conceived him already dead and arranged a funeral with numerous weeping handmaids.

Upon Pelias' arrival, he deemed that the child no longer posed a threat and departed. The baby was sent secretly to Mount Pelion to be trained and protected by the wise centaur Chiron.

One day, on the shores of the sea, along with some of the prince's friends, Pelias spotted a tall, long-haired boy wearing a tight-fitting leather bodice adorned with skin of leopard. He possessed two spears but only one stocking. Some time ago, a soothsayer had foretold Peleas that his death would come the moment he crossed paths with a man with only one stocking. Jason lost that stocking while rescuing an elderly woman unable to cross a river.

Jason carried the woman on his back, but in doing so he lost his sandal. The old woman was none other than Hera, disguised. She wished to take revenge on Pelias, who, among other failings, had forgotten to make a sacrifice in her honor. Pelias immediately introduced himself to him, asking, " Who are you and what is your father's name?" The boy answered quietly, " My name is Jason. My foster father is the wise Chiron, while my real name is Diomedes, son of Aeson."

Pelias shuddered; he thought the young man was dead. Pelias continued talking to him without revealing his origin. He asked him, " What would you say if an oracle predicted that one of your countrymen would lead you to your death?"

"I wouldn't know. I certainly would not be able to eliminate him," Jason replied, "but I would assign him to an unattainable mission, such as going in search of the Golden Fleece in Colchis." Jason could not know it, but it was Hera who put those words into his mouth. And Jason added, "Who am I conversing with anyway?" Pelias finally revealed himself.

Realizing that he was facing the usurper, Jason demanded that the kingdom be returned to him. Pelias, unable to do anything, said, "Okay, I will hand over my kingdom to you since I have now become tired and aged. I want to thank you for this opportunity. But first you must remove the curse that has fallen on Iolcus. The body of Phrixus, which has not been buried in his homeland, must return here, along with the Golden Fleece."

The mission that Pelias entrusted to Jason was a way to keep him away from Iolco, with the hope that on this journey full of pitfalls, Jason would lose his life.

Jason, who could not deny Peleus this favor, sent heralds around Greece in search of valiant companions for this most dangerous voyage. He asked Argos, the most experienced boat-maker, to make him a ship that could have fifty oars. Argos went in search of the finest wood, and it was Athena herself who procured for him fairy wood that came from Dodona. With this wood the figurehead of the great vessel was carved. This meant that the ship was able to converse as if by magic with the sailors who maneuvered it. There were several heroes who acceded to Jason's invitation by hastening to board the fairy ship. Among them were Admetus prince of Pherae, Atalanta of Calydon the virgin hunter, Castor and Pollux the Dioscuri, Hylas helper of Heracles, Lynceus, and Melampius,

Meleager, Peleus the father of Achilles, Orpheus the poet, and many others. Heracles, after catching the boar in one of his labors, suddenly entered the scene, jumping with all his weight onto the ship Argo.
From the beginning, the other Argonauts wanted to entrust the command of the vessel to Heracles, who, however, politely declined such a task and preferred to abide by the orders of Jason, who, despite being very young, was well trained for the expedition. The ship was launched and Jason performed his sacrifices to the deity Apollo. As the smoke from the sacrifices rose into the sky, the Argonauts celebrated and Orpheus quelled the brawls among the drunkards. At first light they set sail and headed for the island of Lemnos, where they would face their first adventure.

But before we go any further, you may be wondering: What was this golden fleece? And who was this Phrixus who died far from home?

Aeolus had several sons, including Sisyphus and Athamas. Athamas married at Zeus's behest Nephele, a cloud nymph, who, again at Zeus's behest, took the form of Hera giving him a son, Phrixus, and a daughter, Helle.

But Athamas forgot his wife by falling in love with Ino, daughter of Cadmus, ruler of Tyre, by whom he had two sons. As soon as Nepheles learned of this, he climbed up on Olympus and complained to Hera, cursing Athamas and her offspring, including her children.

Nepheles tried to deceive Athamas with false prophecies that led to Phrixus' death sentence. Phrixus was a beautiful young man whose aunt Demodice, the second wife of Cretheus the ruler of Iolcus, fell in love with him. The young man rejected his aunt's attentions, and the aunt in revenge accused him of raping her and then demanded that he be killed. Phrixus was therefore sent to death. Athamas, in tears and with death in his heart, took Phrixus to the top of a mountain in order to kill him. In extremis, Heracles arrived and rebuked Athamas for the deed he was about to do, as Zeus did not like human sacrifices, offering Phrixus a way of escape.

A wonderful golden ram, sent by Hermes himself, would rescue the young man.

This special ram was able to fly, so Phrixus could escape from any human threat. The ram stared Phrixus in the eyes and intimated to him, " Get on my back." The beautiful younger sister, Helle, realizing that her father's abode no longer represented a safe place for her, begged her brother to take her with him. So, Phrixus and Helle set out eastward. However, just above the body of water that overlooked the Black Sea, young Helle was overcome by dizziness, let go of her grip and fell into the sea, dying.

In memory of the unfortunate maiden, that stretch of sea is still called Hellespont, better known as Dardanelles, precisely in honor of Phrixus' sister.

Having arrived unharmed in Colchis, Phrixus settled there, poor and alone, but at least alive. The golden skin of the ram offered in sacrifice would become the property of the ruler of those lands, Aeetes, suspended on a tree in the shadow of a dragon that never slept.

At the same time, the Argonauts arrived on Lemnos and were greeted by an unbearable stench. Indeed, the island in question was damned. About a year prior to the arrival of Jason and his companions, the males of the island of Lemnos complained that their women stank. This was probably due to the fact that they produced ford, a plant product for making portraits and dyes that gave off an incredible stench but was highly sought after as a commodity. The men, who were disgusted with their wives, brought concubines to Lemnos who emitted no stench. The women of Lemnos revolted and, brandishing weapons, killed their mates, their sons and their fathers. Thus this island, unbeknownst to anyone in Greece, became one of the few places, outside the capital of the Amazon kingdom, where women ruled.

Their stench spread throughout the island that was the scene of this absurd massacre. The queen, Princess Ipsipila, did not have the courage to kill her father and let him escape just in time, thus allowing him to save his life. As soon as the ship Argo was sighted on the horizon, she ordered all the women to arm themselves. Our protagonists landed but seeing all the women armed, they feared they would have to fight. To calm their spirits, the eloquent argonaut Echion, Jason's herald, intervened. Ipsipila allowed the Argonauts to land at the dock but did not allow them to enter the city for fear that the massacre of men would be revealed. At the council assembled in the capital, Polyxo, Hypsipyle's nurse, made a proposal that was approved by all the women: "To preserve our beloved island of Lemnos from disappearing, the best thing we can do is to give ourselves to these brave adventurers. The offspring that will result will surely be very solid and noble."

Therefore, the Argonauts were let into the city and Jason was told that the men, because of the constant mistreatment of their women, were driven out, forced to emigrate. Ipsipila, eyeing Jason, offered him the throne of Lemnos. Jason refused the gift that was proposed to him since he had to complete the mission of the Golden Fleece, but he did not despise the queen's appreciation at all. From their meeting was born Euneus w h o , having become ruler, would attempt to rid the island of the stench with appropriate sacrifices. The heroes stopped in the arms of multiple lovers, risking the failure of the mission. Only one Argonaut remained on board to guard the ship Argo: Heracles. This hero had always been ready for excess, but on this occasion he was the most cautious of the crew. The clock was ticking and he was beginning to grow impatient, so he leapt onto the dock and, with his mace in hand, knocked on every door to remind his companions to stand guard. So, having embarked the last of his companions, the ship Argo headed for

Samothrace. Good spirits reigned on the sailing ship, so Heracles issued a challenge to his companions in a rowing race.

All the heroes agreed, even though they knew that no one would be able to beat him; and that was what happened. One after another, they gave up rowing. Only the two Dioscuri, Castor and Pollux, and Jason resisted Heracles' pace. At first, it was the two Dioscuri who gave up. Later, in the lands of Misia, Jason fainted from exhaustion. At practically the same time, Heracles' oar broke into several parts. The hero became angry at the oar, which was so fragile that it had taken away his joy in mocking his weak companions. The Argonauts, laughing, quietly rowed again.

They went ashore to stock up on provisions and water. Hylas, Heracles' aide, walked away with jars to fill them

Of water, but he never returned. Heracles, worried, went looking for his companion in the woods, but without finding him. He nearly went mad with anger and sorrow for his missing friend. Hylas, at the spring where he had gone to fill his vessels, was escorted by the nymphs. At first sight they all fell in love with him, as the young man was very handsome and true. With flattery and pampering they seduced him and, once they entered the water, captured him, taking him to the depths of a lake. Heracles, in pain, did not return to the ship to resume his labors.

Jason, together with his companions, continued the journey making a second stop on a peninsula in the kingdom of Cyzicus, ruled by an old friend of his, the ruler Cyzicus. The ruler was so pleased to meet him that he invited him to a wonderful dinner full of all kinds of amusements and joys. In fact, his union with Cleite was being celebrated. So the two friends toasted, laughed, joked and celebrated their great friendship. The inhabitants of that place, despite the joy of that celebration, harbored in their hearts a great fear of the six-armed giants who occasionally made raids robbing and killing. While the crew was at the ruler's celebration, these giants attacked Argos, however, the heroes who had remained to guard the pier were able to thwart them. The next morning, they all, they greeted, embraced and promised each other eternal cooperation.

The sailing ship set out, but a sudden storm came up and so much darkness fell on the ship that Tiphys, the captain, was no longer able to steer it. In the midst of the gale, he spotted a beach and immediately tried to reach it. The Argonauts were not even in time to disembark and feel safe that they were attacked by enemies who emerged from the darkness. Immediately, the Argonauts began to defend themselves and fight blindly in the eerie darkness that surrounded them.

Our protagonists were unaware that the storm had driven them back to the shores they had just left. Those against whom they were fighting were none other than the friends with whom they had feasted a few hours earlier. In the darkness, the people of Cyzicus believed that the corsairs had come from the sea to the point where they were facing them with all their energy.

Meanwhile, the Argonauts, believing they had landed on a remote coast and not recognizing their friends, believed they had fallen into an ambush by an opponent virtually impossible to recognize.

Suddenly, the darkness faded, the light returned, and the friends recognized each other. They realized that a massacre between brothers had occurred and knelt down weeping. Jason, too, disappeared the black cloud, he realized that his great friend, the ruler Cyzicus, died under the blows of his sword.

But how did this happen? The deity Rhea, angry that the city's inhabitants had fought against her six-armed sons, let a black cloud fall over the entire city and the sea. Meanwhile, Pan, the god of the woods, made sure that men did not recognize each other. His power was tremendous; thanks to his voice, Pan was able to cause hallucinations in the eyes of his listeners. Rea's revenge had been realized. All that remained was to bury the fallen and mourn the deaths of dear friends.

The Argo was back at sea and reached the island of Bebryces, where the arrogant ruler Amycus ruled. When the heroes landed, their only intention (after what had happened on the island of Cyzicus) was to distract themselves, have fun, and forget. Amycus, son of Poseidon, was one of the strongest boxers in the world. When he learned that on the 'Argo, among the sailors, was Pollux, one of the two Dioscuri, a boxer as famous as himself, he could not resist the call of the challenge and invited him, therefore, to a fight. Amycus was the son of a deity, and Pollux was a demigod whom no one could beat.

The clash was bloody and continued for a long time, as neither was able to beat the other. Amycus, against all sporting spirit, used gloves with metal spikes of bronze, unlike Pollux who used ordinary gloves. Pollux, quicker and more alert, incensed him by targeting him with powerful and well-aimed blows to the nose and jaw. Still without sportsmanship,

Amycus grabbed his wrist and held him back. He charged a blow, but before he could deliver it, Pollux struck him in his only weak point, his elbow. Hit in the right part, Amycus lost all his strength in an instant and had to succumb to the following three punches from the very strong Pollux.

The next day, the Argonauts set sail again, starting from the island of Bebryces, ruled by the late ruler Amycus, and landed at Salmydessus in southern Thrace, a place where Phineus, son of Agenor, ruled. Phineus possessed a special gift: he was able to predict events with such accuracy as he was dazzled by divine will. In addition, a pair of Harpies, Aello and Ocypete, gave him no respite. These horrible winged beasts would swoop into the palace at mealtime and steal his food from the table, fouling the leftovers with their excrement to make it inedible.

When Jason asked Phineas how they could get hold of the golden fleece, the ruler replied, "I will answer you, but first rid me of the Harpies." Phineas' servants, while talking to Jason, set the royal table to host the Argonauts. But immediately the Harpies arrived and daubed the courses and wines. The two Argonauts Calais and

Zetes, winged sons of Borea, took to the air with their swords and chased the Harpies through the air, forcing them to flee far beyond the sea. Some say the two chased the Harpies all the way to the Strophades Islands, sparing their lives.

The Harpies returned to their cave in Crete and no longer bothered Phineus.

The seer king explained to Jason how to cross the Bosporus. He told Jason precisely where he could find hospitality and what end he would come to on his way to Colchis, the land located in the foothills of the Caucasus Mountains.

Phineas added that once he arrived in Colchis, Jason was to present himself to Aphrodite. The ruler Phineas had married Cleopatra, sister of Calais and Zetes, and, after her demise, Idaea, a princess of Scythia. Idaea, envious of Cleopatra's two sons, hired false witnesses in order to blame them for all sorts of crimes. Calais and Zetes, however, realized the deception, and freed their grandsons, who had been locked up in prison. Phineas not only covered the Argonauts with gifts, but sent the jealous bride back to her father. The ruler Phineas warned the Argonauts of the danger of the Symplegades rocks, which, constantly surrounded by sea mist, posed a threat to ships heading toward the Bosporus. If a ship tried to pass through them, the rocks would engage each other, destroying it.

Following Phineas' suggestion, one of the Argonauts released a dove into the sky that was able to flutter near Argos. This dove anticipated the ship by a few meters and passed in front of the rocks, which suddenly and with a great roar tightened into a fatal grip. The dove managed to escape death by spreading its wings faster and losing only a few feathers from its tail. When the rocks began to separate again, the Argonauts began to row full force, led by Athena and encouraged by Orpheus' lyre. Argos emerged virtually unharmed from the gap, losing only a few ornaments. From that day on, according to a prophecy, the rocks of the Symplegades remained firmly in place.

While staying with King Lycus of Mariandynians, Jason lost two valiant members of his company: Idmon, the ship's prophet who bled to death from a boar attack, and Tiphys, the formidable helmsman of Argos, who fell ill and thus lost his life.

A doubt arises at this point: was there anyone attempting to thwart Jason and his enterprise? From Mariandia, Jason stopped in Sinop. The city was named after the cunning young woman who, a unique case in Greek mythology, succeeded in deceiving Zeus. The beautiful Sinop refused flattery and when Zeus assured her that he would offer her as a gift what she liked best, she opted for virginity.

Sinop spent his existence on the shores of the Black Sea in serene solitude. In this same city, Jason welcomed, as new members of the ship, three acquaintances of Heracles who took him to Themyscira, the main city of the Amazonian kingdom.

Jason continued on his journey, passing the village of Chalybes, which was famous for ironworking and for not cultivating land or raising livestock. He passed another village where it was customary for husbands to moan almost as if they were about to give birth when their wives were in the throes of labor, and yet another village where people lived in huts made of wood mating promiscuously with each other. These civilizations, with such bizarre customs, meant that Argos was about to enter places more and more disturbing every day. Argos passed the island of Philyra, where Kronos lay with Philyra, daughter of Oceanus, giving birth to a half-man, half-horse cub, the one who would later be recognized as the wise centaur Chiron.

Soon the Caucasus mountain range appeared, towering over the heads of the Argonauts. Eventually they reached the mouth of the great river that washed the Colchis.

Having arrived, Jason had Argos hide and organized his war council. The question he put to everyone's attention was, "Now that we have finally arrived, will we ask with gracefully to the ruler Aeetes the golden fleece or shall we conquer it by fighting?"

On the island of Ares, flocks of birds flew over Argos, dropping bronze feathers. One of these feathers struck Oileo on the shoulder. The Argonauts immediately covered their heads with their helmets and began to scream with all the voice in their bodies. Part of them of them continued rowing while the rest defended them with their shields. These were probably the birds of Stymphalus, driven away by Heracles in one of his labors. But why this small step back in our history? Because, according to the predictions of the ruler Phineas, the Argonauts had landed on the island of Ares.

They did not have time to anchor before a tremendous storm swept over the sea sweeping four sailors onto the shore. These were Cytisorus, Argo, Phronto and Melas. They were the sons of Phrixus and Chalciope, daughter of King Aeetes of Colchis, and therefore were close relatives of many Argonauts. Jason gathered the four castaways into the ranks of his crew/army.

Gathering the war council, meanwhile that Argos was safely tucked away, Jason was forced to consider that his new fellow adventurers had a shared duty in their hearts: to honor the memory of his father Phrixus, rightful owner of the fleece, or they would go against the wishes of his grandfather Aeetes, who was proud to have inherited it. Precisely why, in the end, Jason's choice was to opt for a diplomatic request. Meanwhile, on Olympus, the goddesses Hera and Athena were anxious about how to help Jason in his venture. They were certain that Aeetes would not deliver the fleece to him. Thus, they turned to Aphrodite for a remedy. Aphrodite sent Eros to shoot one of her arrows into the heart of Medea, the daughter of King Aeetes, to make her enamored of Jason. Medea was an intriguing and fearsome character in mythology, a sorceress who could bend reality through her powers, capable of terrifying, unpredictable and unforgivable actions. Getting her to fall in love with Jason was the stratagem the goddesses decided to implement so that their will would be granted.

Jason and his companions set out and arrived in the capital through the cemetery of the Colchids. The Colchids buried only the bodies of the women, while those of the men were suspended on plants for the birds to devour. Welcoming the heroes was Calicope, daughter of the ruler Aeetes, who, recognizing the young men who had escaped the shipwreck, thanked Jason and his men for leading them home. The ruler also welcomed them, thanking them for saving the lives of his grandchildren. However, once he learned the reason for the visit, he enjoined them to get out of his sight or they would return home with severed hands and tongues.

Jason was not at all concerned: he responded courteously to the ruler Aeetes, who, regretting his abnormal fury, began to negotiate the sale of the fleece, on his own terms. He subjected Jason to unimaginable trials, with the certainty that the young Greek would die trying to pass them.

King Aeetes' palace was made of bronze. Hephaestus himself built it. One of Hephaestus' gifts to this people was a pair of bulls with bronze hooves, spitting fire from their nostrils. The job assigned to Jason was to tie up two bulls, plow a field consecrated to the god Ares and sow dragon's teeth in it. Jason was interjected for a moment, but agreed to the test with a smile on his face. Medea was astonished at his behavior, observing him with deep admiration. At that very instant, an arrow from Olympus struck his heart, and from that moment on, Medea, the terrible avenging and impetuous sorceress, would never again be able to take her eyes off Jason. She vowed to favor him on the condition that he would choose her as his bride. Jason promised the gods that he would always remain faithful to her. The pact in question was made. The young woman gave him an ointment made from a Caucasian flower that was said to have sprouted through the blood of Prometheus. Protected by this ointment Jason, impassive to the fire of the bulls, managed to entangle them and make them work in Ares' camp. Again on Medea's advice, Jason carefully scattered the dragon's teeth in the plowed field. Immediately men sprang up, completely armed, who warily set out toward Jason. The protagonist was not intimidated because Medea had adequately prepared him for the conflict. She threw large boulders among their ranks, and the soldiers, disturbed by these boulders, thinking that each was being attacked by his neighbor, began to duel among themselves.

The very few survivors surrendered to Jason's military might. The ruler Aeetes went back on his word and refused to give Jason the fleece he had been promised-or rather, he ordered the Argonauts to leave immediately. In his anger, he threatened to burn the ship and have his army slaughter the heroes. But the ruler Aeetes made a mistake: he confessed to Medea the place where the golden fleece was hidden.

Medea, hopelessly in love with our hero Jason, led him to the secret enclosure of Ares outside the city. There, the fleece hung on an oak tree and was guarded by a dragon who never rested. It was impossible for anyone to approach the fleece except Medea. Through mysterious spells, she calmed the beast by putting it to sleep. Removing the golden fleece from the oak was thus easier. Immediately Jason, with Medea and his companions , ran to the ship, for the alarm was immediately raised. The priests of Ares, with weapons in their fists, chased after them, wounding Iphitos, Melager, Atalanta and Jason himself. They all managed to get on board just in time.

Because of their severe wounds, Iphitos lost his life; in contrast, Jason and the others healed quickly thanks to the miraculous dressings of Medea, who could not stay in her father's house because she had betrayed her father for love. In extremis, Absyrtus, Medea's little brother, also embarked.

At this point Argos was returning home, chased by the swift ship of King Aeetes. Argo was proceeding fast on the northern shore of the Black Sea, but Aeetes' ships, which were following the Argonauts, were growing more and more menacing. By now she had been joined by the flagship, with the ruler Aeetes himself in command. The Argonauts were preparing for an unequal fight. Medea, in the presence of her father, who was cursing her from his boat, killed Absyrtus by cutting his body into a thousand pieces. Before the horrified eyes of her father, who was dumbfounded, she threw the pieces into the sea, one by one, forcing the desperate ruler to stop his chase and pick them up before they disappeared forever. This terrible gesture temporarily saved the Argonauts from pursuit but scarred the entire crew, so that from then on, according to various accounts, they found themselves wandering all over the seas of Europe. The ship Argo also refused to return home with Jason and Medea on board until the two were freed, cleansed of this murder. To do so, they would have to land at the island of the sorceress

Circe, Medea's aunt, who would provide this purification.
Some returned Argos to the Danube and then back to the sea using the waters of the Po River. Others made Argos enter Finland in the sea from which the Danube was believed to have originated and then return to the Mediterranean from the Pillars of Heracles.
They also stopped at the island of Elba, to which they assigned the name Argo. The drops of sweat that fell on the beach from the Argonauts' foreheads turned into metal crystals. Some made the Argo transit the Don River, causing it to flow into the Indian Gulf.

However, these are only accounts that want to implicate Jason in the different mythologies. It is more plausible that Jason crossed the straits of the Dardanelles. Troy, a stupendous city, once a formidable sentinel to the passage, no longer constituted an eventual slowdown, as Heracles, crossing it, sank the Trojan ships one by one. Our heroes then landed on an island, accepting the hospitality of the ruler Alcinous. The pursuers also landed suddenly but, under the law of hospitality, could do nothing.

They sent a representation to ask the ruler to return the fugitives Medea and Jason, as well as the fleece to the troops of the ruler Aeetes. Alcinous replied that he would issue his sentence the next day. Arete, Alcinoo's daughter, who had become friends with Medea, had her father tell her what his real intentions were. Alcinoo wanted to return his daughter to her father if she turned out to still be a virgin the next day. This meant that the union between the two young lovers had not yet taken place and, therefore, Medea would still be considered her father's property and not Jason's. That same night, Jason married Medea in a cave named after the nymph who raised and fed the baby Dionysus there.

Jason and Medea lay together as husband and wife on the well-spread golden fleece. The next morning the Colchids, given recent events and unable to complete the task of returning the fugitives to Colchis for fear of the ruler Aeetes, decided not to return home. The Argonauts resumed sailing, skirting the island of the Sirens who tried to lure and then kill them. The sirens' song was suppressed by the sound of Orpheus' lyre, who won the challenge. Many of them would commit suicide in defeat, while others would take refuge in mysterious places. New generations of sirens would attempt to enchant Odysseus, who would be tied securely to the ship's mast to avoid diving into the sea in pursuit of the sirens. A gale dragged Argos out of the

Sicily but it was with the help of Orpheus, who advised the Argonauts to pray to the god Triton that the latter would lead them back to a navigable waterway.

In return, the god obtained a tripod, which from then on became his symbol. Jason possessed two tripods and decided to give the second one as a gift to the people of Libya. To thank him for the gift, the god guaranteed that one day a descendant of the Argonauts would return to those lands, take possession of that tripod, and become lord of all North Africa. Out of fear, the people buried that tripod, which is still patiently waiting to be unearthed by a descendant of the Argonauts.

Once again on course, they tried to land on Crete, but there they found Talos, a bronze behemoth who watched over the island by scampering on the beaches and throwing stones at ships trying to dock. Nothing could hurt him. This colossus, created by Hephaestus himself, had a very fragile little vein. And in fact, at one foot was a nail that protected it.

Medea was aware of this and deluded the giant by promising him eternal life if he drank her potion. But the potion was a powerful sedative, and once Talos dozed off, Medea brought out the nail, thus causing the end of the guardian of Crete.

Following a few more stops, Argo arrived in Iolcus one autumn evening, but there was no one to welcome them to the beach. Word had spread in Thessaly that they were dead. This news had also reached the ears of the ruler Pelias. Strong in the knowledge that Jason would never return to reclaim the throne and free his captive father, Pelias ordered the killing of the hero's entire family. Aeson, Jason's father, obtained permission to kill himself by drinking the blood of a bull. Alcimedes pierced himself with a sword after cursing Pelias who, a moment earlier, had smashed the head of Promachus, Jason's brother, born shortly after the departure of the ship Argo. Jason, having learned all this, ordered the faithful servant who had given him this news not to reveal the arrival of Argo so that he could prepare his revenge.

There was a new council of war. There was no discussion about whether to attack Iolcus or not. Acastus, one of the Argonauts, was the son of Pelias and could not march against his father. Moreover, Jason could not attack the city he intended to rule. Medea stepped in and declared that she had a plan. All they would have to do was wait a few hours, hiding in the woods. As soon as they saw the light of a flashlight appear on the royal palace, they could enter Iolcus without drawing their swords. Medea ordered two maidens to put on the priestess robes of the goddess and headed for the gates of Iolcus.

But before gaining access and facing the sentries, Medea turned into an old woman, asking to pass and confer with the ruler Pelias, even though it was late at night. The goddess Artemis sent him a message. Pelias hurried to let the old woman in with the statue brought by the priestesses. Medea claimed to be the bearer of the gift of youth that the goddess of the hunt had agreed to give to King Pelias. Rejuvenation, however, required a series of precise actions. Pelias asked what these actions were. Medea had an old half-blind goat brought in, killed it, cut it into thirteen pieces and threw the pieces into a cauldron boiling over the fire, shouting, "The power of Artemis is enormous." Medea then pulled a lamb out of a cavity in the statue of Artemis, which began to leap around the room.

Pelias, persuaded by the procedure, allowed himself to be put to sleep by the magic of Medea, who ordered that Pelias' three daughters-Alcestis, Evadne, and Anphinome-shred their father and then throw the various parts into the cauldron. Alcestis refused to perform such an unnatural action, while the other two obeyed by killing their father. After the body was thrown into the cauldron, Medea ordered the two to go with flashlights to pray to Artemis on the palace terrace. At that signal, Jason entered the city and found all the inhabitants in religious fury praying to Artemis-another spell of Medea's. The throne was his, but he did not desire it more. He left the kingdom to Acastus and, being the husband of the one who had the king killed, was banished from Iolco. Jason and Medea therefore, decided to leave those lands immediately. Their story continued ... but here ends the long and magical journey on the ship Argo.

Jason and Medea lived happily in Corinth for ten years, warmly welcomed by King Creon; but then Jason fell in love with the king's daughter, Princess Creusa, and repudiated Medea...

How Jason could have dared so much, knowing too well the ferocity of his wife's reactions, is unknown.

His mind was darkened by love, and Medea's revenge was not long in coming. Furious at her husband's ingratitude and betrayal, Medea sent Creusa a poisoned robe that killed her and her father, who had rushed to her aid, with atrocious suffering. Then, after killing the two sons she had had by Jason, Medea fled to Athens in a winged chariot that the god Helios, her grandfather, had provided for her.

In Athens, the wicked sorceress married, as we know, the king of the Aegean, father of Theseus, whom she also tried to poison. After being discovered, she went, together with Aegeus' son Medus, to a distant region of Asia called Media. Finally, Medea returned to Colchis with her father. The glorious Jason ended his days miserably, crushed by the hull of the ship Argo, which had placed on the isthmus of Corinth as propitiatory offering to the god Poseidon.

Chapter 3
Greek deities

3.1 Zeus

According to Greek mythology, Zeus, in addition to being the most important god among all deities, was also the celestial god who guaranteed light and heat. Any atmospheric phenomenon depended on him. He was even the ruler of thunder, light and heat. Also through the use of thunder and lightning he manifested his approval or disapproval.

His abode was Olympus, from which he governed the totality of the universal order. The fate of all men was in his hands, although his decisions were subject to a higher will: that of Fate, whose rules and decisions could not be changed even by the powerful ruler of the gods. Mythology relates that he was born to Rhea and Kronos and, through various vicissitudes, ousted his father Kronos and became the ruler of the gods. He had several brides and mistresses. The first was Meti. Later, he married Themis, Dione, Maia, Demeter, Persephone, Eurinome, Mnemosyne, and Leto, all of whom were later repudiated for one reason or another (although numerous historians disagree that he "formalized" his position with all of them). Ultimately, he married his sister Hera.

To make a long story short, one must think that we are all children of Zeus! Because of these constant vicissitudes, scholars tell of him perpetually quarreling with his wife Hera, but he never parted with her.

During his national holiday, the Olympic Games were held, in which all the countries of Greece took part. In the city of Olympia, there was the most beautiful temple consecrated to him, in which there was the famous statue of the god executed by Phidias, made of ivory and gold (unfortunately, nothing remains of it, but it was considered among the seven wonders of the world). The symbols of Zeus were the eagle, scepter and thunderbolt; he was depicted as a mighty and austere man.

3.2 Poseidon

Poseidon was the son of Kronos and Rhea and older brother of Zeus. He was identified as the ruler of the sea and the father of the waters. The worship of Poseidon was very prominent in ancient Greece, taking into account the fact that Greeks were mostly sailors and fishermen. He was also believed to be the god of earthquakes. Poseidon lived in a palace submerged by the waters with his trident (made for him by Hephaestus), which had the power to appease or agitate the sea. Poseidon's wife was Amphitrite, a sea deity, but he had(like his younger brother Zeus) numerous mistresses and many children. From union with his wife were born Triton, Benthesikyme and Rhodes; from a casual relationship with Demeter was born the famous horse Arion; and from a love affair with the nymph Those was born the Cyclops Polyphemus, to name a few. For Poseidon, the bull, the horse and the dolphin were sacred animals. Even the pine tree which although not an animal represented something sacred to Poseidon.

3.3 Ade

Hades, in Hellenic mythology, was the son of Kronos and Rhea, brother of Zeus and Poseidon, honored and worshipped as the lord and master of the realm of the dead whose court consisted of such fearsome creatures as the demons of death (Thanatos) the demons of sleep (Hypnos), the demons of violent death on the battlefield (Keres), the demons of blizzard violence (Harpies), the demons of regret and divine blasphemy (Erinyes), and many more.

Hades' presence, moreover, had not only a baleful significance, but was also believed to be a bringer of riches hidden in the earthly womb. Hades was said to be so ugly that every woman fled from his sight. Therefore, when he became infatuated with Persephone, he was obliged to capture her since he was concerned about her probable rejection. Hades possessed a helmet that made him invisible when worn. Perseus, for example, used it to eliminate Medusa.

3.4 Hera

According to Greek mythology, Hera was the sister of Zeus as the daughter of Kronos and Rhea (according to Hesiod, his seventh wife). With Zeus she gave birth to four children, Ares, Hephaestus, Eilezia and Hebe. Jealous of her husband, who had Athena without her, Hera created the colossus Typhon without the help of her spouse. The woman was known in antiquity not only because of her jealousy and rivalry against Zeus' many wives, but also by virtue of her loveliness and worship of herself. She is known to have persecuted Paris and all the Trojans because Paris preferred Aphrodite to him. She also persecuted her husband's many mistresses. However, in time, Hera became the symbol of conjugal love, the guardian of marital warmth and bonding and of all the most important events in a woman's life. She became in practice the symbol of feminine qualities. The pomegranate was sacred to Hera, and among the animals the peacock, crow and cuckoo.

3.5 Demeter

Demeter, daughter of Kronos and Rhea, and therefore also sister of Zeus, in Greek mythology represented the deity of plants and grains and undisputed protector of the fertility of the soil and also of female fertility. Demeter gave birth to two children: Persephone, whom she had with her brother Zeus, and Pluto, deity of prosperity, whom she had with the mortal Iasion. In addition to these, she gave birth to the horse Arion thanks to her brother Poseidon, as Demeter had turned into a filly to escape him. At that point, Poseidon transformed himself into a horse in order to succeed in taking possession of her. Demeter's main place of worship was the city of Eleusis where the Eleusias and Thesmophoras were celebrated in her honor.

3.6 Hestia

Hestia, according to Hellenic mythology, was the goddess of flames seen in their beneficent aspect. Daughter of Kronos and Rhea and sister of Zeus, from whom she received consent to remain a virgin at all times and to be the guardian of the hearth and domestic peace. She was harassed by Apollo and Poseidon, who wanted to marry her. In ancient texts, Hestia first appeared in Hesiod's Theogony and Homeric hymns. Hestia was a deity who was also honored in temples where sacred fire was kept. Several shrines were dedicated to her, including the most famous: the one at Delphi, from which the Greeks extracted the sacred fire when leaving to found new colonies.

3.7 Apollo

Apollo, was the son of Zeus and Leto and the twin brother of Artemis. He was considered the solar deity par excellence, god of all things beautiful, including music, art, and poetry. He also guided and protected the muses, wayfarers and sailors. He was considered the prophet of Zeus because of his divinatory faculties. As a solar god, he also bore the name Phoebus (he who spends, who illuminates) and traveled across the sky in a chariot of gold and gems, drawn by four horses whose nostrils emitted fire. But Apollo was also a warrior god, the sower of death and destruction, as Homer records in the first book of the Iliad. Apollo loved many women, including Daphne, and also two young men (Cyparissus and Hyacinth). Pythian games were celebrated in his honor in Greece. Animals sacred to Apollo were the wolf and the swan and, among plants, the laurel and the olive tree.

3.8 Artemis

The goddess Artemis, in Greek mythology, represented a very problematic figure. She was the daughter of Zeus and Leto and twin sister of Apollo. She was born on the island of Delos. In contrast to Apollo, a deity who represented the sun, Artemis was the goddess who represented the moon. She is most commonly identified as the goddess of the hunt, who, armed with bows and arrows, and followed by her troop of nymphs, roamed the mountains and meadows in search of prey, sparing not the brave who dared to face her. Goddess of chastity, she protected maidens until marriage. Her veneration as a lunar deity was sometimes linked to Hecate and, in some localities, she was celebrated as the deity of married women and childbirth. The goddess, according to myth, was also considered a deity of fishing and navigation. For this reason, she was highly revered and respected in Crete.

In Arcadia, she was considered the progenitor of the people and honored as Agrotera (deity of untamable nature). A completely different thing happened in Ephesus, where this deity was considered the protector of nature. Her cult was so strong and deep-rooted that it remained until the beginning of the Christian era. Some scholars trace its origin to the Amazons.

3.9 Hermes

Hermes, son of Zeus and the nymph Maia, was one of the most famous deities in Greek mythology. He came to light in a cave on Mount Cyllene in Arcadia.

As time went on, Hermes became the guardian of travelers and their trade, including honest and dishonest sellers, hence his reputation as the defender of thieves. Because merchants had to talk a lot, Hermes was also referred to as the god of eloquence and the courier of the gods. This was a deity who had to move a lot to fulfill his duties, so he was also the defender and protector of sportsmen. But his duties did not end there; at night, in fact, when men and gods did not need his services, he became the god who accompanied the shadows of the dead to their new abode (hence, the appellation Psychopompus).

Hermes' exploits were so numerous that we find some of them in every myth. He gave Perseus a hand in killing Medusa; he interceded with Hades to free Persephone; and many others.

Recall, among his creations, the lyre he created for Apollo (who, in turn, gave it to Orpheus by emptying the shell of a tortoise and putting in the well-preserved entrails of an ox. Orpheus obtained as a gift from Apollo the famous golden rod (which later became the staff of eloquence in the

Hermes' hands). Hermes obtained his famous winged hat as a gift from Zeus, as well as a pair of sandals with wings so that he could perform Zeus' tasks more quickly. As Zeus' courier, Hermes also had the task of carrying men's dreams, as they were believed to be sent to Zeus. Despite this great task, Hermes still managed to carve out some time to fall in love: Together with Aphrodite he begat Hermaphroditus; he loved Penelope before she became Odysseus' wife and from her he had the god Pan (according to some accounts); and many others. The festivals called Hermaea were organized in honor of Hermes.

3.10 Dionysus

Dionysus was the most important earthly deity in Hellenic mythology. Dionysus was the only deity who did not possess two gods as parents. His father was Zeus and his mother was the mortal Semele, daughter of Cadmus, ruler of Thebes. Once pregnant, Semele died prematurely. Zeus extracted Dionysus from her womb and sewed him back into a thigh, in which he held Dionysus until his birth. He was best known as the god of wine, as it is said that he invented the art of its production and o f working the earth in such a way as to bring the fruit to maturity. As time went on, he also became famous as the god of saving, civilization, and also of joy and happiness. He was credited with the art of divination and the ability to cure evils.

Dionysus was also a god with a complicated character. We find him pitiful and merciful, for example, toward Ariadne and Pan, while at times he was also a provocateur, as with Orpheus. His cult spread throughout Greece and Asia Minor. Dionysian festivals were held in his honor, and his influence on draughtsmen, men of letters, artists, sculptors, and painters was enormous, according to the countless records handed down to us through poems, tragic works, statues, and frescoes. Depending on the times and the artist, he was depicted in different ways: sometimes as a handsome young man, sometimes as a bearded and robust man, and sometimes as an obese old man and curmudgeonly. It was often adorned with branches, bunches of grapes and ivy. The vine and ivy were sacred to Dionysus, as were the following animals: the goat, tiger, lynx, lion, and dolphin.

3.11 Ares

Ares was the son of Zeus and Hera or, according to other versions, of Hera alone, who, envious that Zeus had given birth to Athena alone, conceived him while sitting on a flower pointed out by the nymph Flora. Ares, who was defined as the fierce and ruthless god of war, was raised by the goddess Enyo, a deity who embodied all the ruthlessness, brutality and violence of war.

Ares was also known because whenever he left for battle, he was always flanked by his sons, Deimos, Phobos, and Eris. During the Trojan War, he sided with the Trojans and was wounded by Diomedes, to whom Athens oriented the auction. In spite of his ferocity, he fell madly in love with Aphrodite and, by Zeus' order, the two were united in marriage, giving birth to five children. He had many earthly mistresses, but Aphrodite was his dearest bride. Ares was an object of veneration only among the Thracians, who were thought to be a people of warriors and savages. He had several temples consecrated to him in Thebes, however.

3.12 Aphrodite

In Greek mythology, Aphrodite represented the goddess of beauty and love. Homer supported the hypothesis that she was born of Zeus and Dione, but the most common theory is that of Hesiod, according to which she arose from the mists of the sea fertilized by the genitals of Uranus. She was the wife of the terrible Hephaestus by the will of Zeus, yet she experienced many adventures, both with other deities (Ares, Eros, Hermes, Poseidon and others) and with mortals (Adonis, Anchises, from whom she had Aeneas, etc.). Aphrodite was an extremely complex deity but one who, in any case, always represented the value of 'love in all its different manifestations aimed at preserving life. In this respect, her cult was very heterogeneous: in some villages they worshipped Aphrodite to obtain pure and sincere love such as that between young people. In other parts of Greece, however, she was worshiped as a deity of sex and unbridled passion that knows no bounds. The deity considered three plants sacred: t h e myrtle, rose, apple tree, and poppy. Sacred animals, on the other hand, were the dove, sparrow, swan, hare, goat, tortoise, and dolphin.

3.13 Athena

Athena was born of Zeus. Aside from being the warrior goddess, Athena was the goddess of rationality, the arts, philosophy and literature, the marketplace and industry. She taught men to travel, plow land, raise oxen and ride horses. She taught women to sew, weave, dye and embroider. She was also a proud goddess who harshly punished those who dared to compete against her.

As a warrior goddess, Athena was in opposition to Ares, the personification of brutal and violent warfare. From her comes the name of the city of Athens, Greece, since she gave the olive tree to the city.

She is said to have invented the quadriga and the war chariot, as well as olive oil and its use in Attica. Athena, as a warrior goddess, participated in numerous adventures. She sided with her father in the battle against the Titans; she was the judge of the dispute between Aphrodite and Hera; she allied herself with the Greeks during the Trojan War; following the fall of Troy, she favored Odysseus in his vicissitudes; she directed the construction of the ship Argo; she assisted Perseus in his battle against Medusa; and many other exploits.

One of the many legends states that, one day, Tiresias passed the goddess while bathing and observed her naked in all her extreme magnificence. Athena, as soon as she realized being spied on, she became so enraged that she made Tiresias blind. However, regretting her act, she bestowed upon him the gift of prophecy. From that day was born the legend of Tiresias, the old blind man, the greatest among the soothsayers existing in ancient times. To Athena, the rooster and the owl were sacred beasts.

3.14 Hephaestus

Hephaestus, in Greek mythology, represented the deity of earthly fire seen in a good sense: fire as an element of civilization. According to most experts, he was the son of Zeus and Hera, although for Hesiod he was born only to Hera, who, at the sight of such a horrible son, hurled him down from the sky. He fell on a mountain, where he remained for nine years hidden in a cave, cared for by Thetis and Eurynome. That cave was said to be his first blacksmith's workshop. Once he became an adult, Hephaestus created a splendid throne, which he gave to his mother, Hera. After various events, he became so loving that he never stopped defending her. One day Zeus became angry because Hephaestus was always protecting his mother, so he banished him from Olympus. Hephaestus fell on the island of Lemnos. According to some, it was as a result of this fall that he became an invalid.

In any case, Hephaestus is known as a great blacksmith: the creator of the chariot of the sun, the lightning bolt and scepter of Zeus, the golden armor of Heracles, the helmet of Ares, the armor of Achilles and Aeneas, the trident of Poseidon, and many others. Paradoxically, Hephaestus, the ugliest of gods, had, as his wife Aphrodite, the most beautiful among goddesses. Even the creation of the first woman, Pandora, on Zeus' commission, was her work.

Chapter 4
Greek myths

4.1 The chains of Prometheus

"Prometheus the wise Titan of cunning and perverse thought, who always remained faithful to his human son-in-law."

Zeus, after becoming ruler of immortals and non-immortals, stopped dealing directly with humankind, leaving them to their fate.

The only one who opposed this was Prometheus, and it was to his credit that the mortals did not disperse.

Prometheus frequently went to earth to bring comfort to men, who at that time still dwelt in a savage state. Unaware of the most basic knowledge and the cyclical nature of time, men dwelt in caves, like ants.

Prometheus showed them how to use wood, lay bricks and make houses. He taught them how to raise flocks, tie oxen to a plow and work the fields. He created the first chariots and boats. He illustrated to men the study of astronomy, the times when the stars rise and set, and the cycles of the moon and sun. He taught men to reason and educated them in the graphic signs that preserve knowledge of things. He indicated to men what medicinal plants were and how to prepare mixtures, ointments and solutions to cure various ailments. He revealed to ordinary mortals the secret gifts of the earth and how to use metals.

He presented mankind with the first insights into social and ethical issues.

First, Prometheus explained the many expressions of the art of divination, unveiled the gloomy voices of omens, propitiatory encounters, and instructed men in the interpretation of their dreams. He first distinguished the flights of predatory birds, and how to derive good omens from them. He introduced the practice of sacrifices to the deity and taught them how to interpret the entrails of beasts sacrificed on altars. He led the hidden eyes of earthlings to the clear auspices of the flames, showing them how to obtain deep and arcane knowledge from them.

All that men know was taught by Prometheus. Beginning in the early Bronze Age, a dispute arose in the city of Mecon between men and some immortals. At that time, after slaughtering an ox, to make peace between the parties, Prometheus intervened. On the one hand, he put the meat and the most valuable parts, wrapping them in the stomach of the animal, so as to make a very unpleasant heap; on the other hand, by a clever ruse, he piled up the bones of the ox, concealing them under an appetizing covering of white fat. In this way, Prometheus attempted to deceive Zeus.

"My dear Prometheus, the most illustrious of all rulers, you have unjustly divided the parts!" Zeus admonished him.

And Prometheus, because of his evil intentions, conscious of his mockery, answered him with a slight sneer, "O Zeus, the most illustrious of the illustrious, choose one of the two sides, the one you like best!"

As he presented the deception to him, Zeus lifted the white fat with both hands and became very angry, in his heart, as soon as he glimpsed the white ox bones put there to mock him.

"Prometheus, wise among wise men, I note with pleasure that you have not lost your urge to mock the immortals!"

From that day on earth, men began to set on fire for the gods the snow-white bones of victims over incense-scented altars, consuming all their flesh.

"Therefore, consume your meat, consume it raw!" Zeus concludes, outraged by the mockery.

Before that time, the lives of human beings had been rather easy: they received the necessities in a single day, remaining idle for the rest of the year. But Zeus, annoyed by Prometheus' deception, concealed from humans the tools for living a comfortable life, and from that day labor and toil became an integral part of the world.

Moreover, until then, human beings, unable to generate fire on their own, drew on the flame of ash trees struck by lightning. From that time, Zeus no longer bestowed his gift on the mortal beings, who remained in the cold and dark, completely deprived of the indefatigable energy of fire.

Always a friend of mankind, Prometheus devised a stratagem to rob the gods of the secret of fire. According to some, he subtracted the flame directly from the abode of Zeus. Others claim, however, that since he could not get to the mountain of Olympus, where Kratos and Bia guarded the residences of the supreme god, Prometheus went to the island of Lemnos, where Hephaestus kept his forge.

The titan seized the sparks of fire and, hidden in a furnace barrel, delivered them to the mortals. From that moment, our progenitors were able to grasp the secret of fire and stopped shivering from the cold and fear of the night as Prometheus was about to face the vengeance of the gods.

Indeed, Zeus' punishment was not long in coming. Prometheus was led to the extreme and deserted limits of Scythia, to the cliffs of Mount Caucasus.

According to some, Zeus bound Prometheus to a pillar with unbreakable laces. Others say that it was the sons of Styx, the implacable Kratos and Bia, who dragged Prometheus to the place of execution, while Hephaestus was instructed to bind him to the rock.

Although Prometheus had stolen fire in his own factory, Hephaestus was not happy with the order given to him by Zeus. It was disgusting for him to carry out such violence against a man of his own origin. But he dared not refuse the supreme god's orders. He turned to Prometheus and said, "You have worshipped men, and this is the consequence. You do not bow to the wrath of the gods; you have honored men as gods, in spite of the law.

And now you will watch the sad stone straight and sleepless, but without kneeling down and cry out in anguish and wailing to the sky without being heard."

Kratos and Bia repeatedly asked Hephaestus to decide and obey. They stayed there to make sure the work was done properly. The gods fastened iron rings around Prometheus' wrists and ankles, and wove iron belts around his chest and waist, thus securing the chains to the rocks so that they could not be loosened.

After the sad assignment, Hephaestus walked away. Kratos and Bia took one last look at Prometheus.

"Outrage now! Depredit even the secrets of the deities now! Give them to those who die only once! Are mortal gods here to soothe your suffering? Those who called you Prometheus, the seer, lied.

All it would take is someone who can figure out how to free you from these chains, but it doesn't exist."

As soon as Zeus's two ruthless bodyguards departed, Prometheus said:

"Divine sky, breaths of wind, swift wings of wind, fountains of river, infinite smile of the sea, Earth queen of all, and with thee, eye of the sun that sees all, I implore thee! Behold a god who suffers gods.

Behold what pain devours me undeservedly and will mar me in time, for endless years..."

He added:

"I can neither keep silent nor shout out my fate, my existence. With mortals I owe a debt, a great divine privilege: for this reason, I was put in chains by my fate. I found the secret of the fire that is hidden in the heart of the reed, lord of all art, the master way that is revealed . This was the sin for which I must pay my sentence, chained and stuck with my face to heaven!

Look at the chained and aching god, the dangerous adversary of Zeus, the most hated by all the gods, who dared to pass through the gates of Zeus' palace because he loved mortals beyond belief!

Not content with such a terrible punishment, Zeus instigated a great-winged eagle, daughter of Echidna and Typhon, against him. Daily, the bird of prey descended on him and devoured pieces of his liver. At night, Prometheus' liver grew back.

The cries of Oceanus and the sea nymphs had no effect; the vengeance of the lord of all gods was implacable and knew no mercy.

Prometheus, however, never stooped to ask for mercy from his executioner; rather, he cried out to the heavens that one day Zeus, too, would have to relinquish his throne if he joined in a fateful marriage with a goddess capable of giving birth to a son stronger than himself. The "prescient" knew the name of the woman who could give birth to such a powerful being, but he would never have revealed her name if Zeus had not first decided to release him.

But this occurred much later, at the hands of Heracles.

4.2 Pandora's Box

A gift, a "magnificent evil," would complete Zeus' revenge on mankind. Pandora, splendid in her ornaments, was welcomed by the uncaring Epimetheus, thus bringing the fragile but fatal female race into the lives of men.

He was certainly not happy, Zeus, seeing fire shining from afar on the earth. With contempt, he turned to Prometheus, who had been chained to his cliff, stating:

"Son of Iapetus, you who are the most ingenious of all, rejoice in stealing fire and avoiding my commands. However, you have reserved a great displeasure for yourself and for those who will follow. To these, as punishment for the stolen fire, I will bestow an evil that all will rejoice in their hearts, gladly welcoming their condemnation." This said, sneeringly, the father of both men and gods.

Immediately Zeus ordered Hephaestus, to mix earth with water and shape a silhouette very much resembling in face and body the immortal goddesses, and to instill in it human voice and splendor. He told Athena to teach her how to weave the cloth, and he told the golden Aphrodite to pour around her head the beauty, heart-rending desires and loving pains that weaken the limbs. But she ordered Hermes, her own herald, to assign her a deceitful nature and a brazen heart.

so ruled Zeus, and immediately the immortals carried out Zeus' order. In a short time, Hephaestus fashioned out of the earth a creature resembling a second maiden, and Athena gave the creature her belt, adorned her with a white robe, and brought down a veil that she had abundantly adorned, marveling at her. The Charites and the venerable Peitho (persuasion) put gold necklaces on her; the beautiful Horae crowned her with spring flowers. The ever-blue-eyed Athena, after placing beautiful garlands of fresh meadow flowers on top of her head, added a golden crown, which Hephaestus had created with his own hands. On it, he had chiseled a large number of representations of strange and terrible beasts.

Ultimately, Hermes placed in the maiden's chest falsehoods and speeches of seduction, and a mischievous temper. Zeus gave her a "pythos," the vase with the advice not to open it. Eventually he gave her the gift of speech, naming her Pandora for the first time, just as all the inhabitants of Olympus gave her their gifts - but probably, with deceptive meaning, as the gods gave her as a gift to human beings, for the eternal failure of humankind.

And the moment Hephaestus finished, rather than a good thing, the splendid evil, he brought Pandora, overflowing with the ornaments given to her by Athena, to where the gods and men were. Surprise seized the immortals and mortals at seeing the fatal deception, with no remedy for human beings. Zeus immediately ordered Hermes to take Pandora to Epimetheus.

Attracted by the girl's caresses, the misguided Titan forgot the recommendation his brother Prometheus had given him in his time: do not, under any circumstances, welcome a tribute from Zeus, but send it back, so as not to harm mortals. Instead, Epimetheus married Pandora, and belatedly realized his mistake.

Removing the huge lid from the jar she had with her, Pandora scattered all the evils it contained over the earth. If until that day human descendants had dwelt on the earth without the annoying diseases that caused infirmity and death, from then on all sorts of problems of a painful nature spilled over to all mankind.

At the bottom of that unbreakable vase, Elpis, the hope, stood alone, unable to get out since Pandora was able to close the lid of the vase again, by order of Zeus.

In contrast, misfortunes, in unlimited quantity, came upon mortals, invading the land and the sea. Diseases struck men both by day and by night, in silence, for Zeus took away their speech. It was not possible to escape Zeus' will.

Until that day, humans were born falling from ash trees, like ripe fruit. However, with Pandora, Zeus gave mankind the female gender, an evil that men accepted with great joy. The delicate and fatal female race originated with Pandora, who went to dwell with men, harassing them with her demands and harassment. Just as the drones remained in the hives in the 'shade, while the bees toiled all day, until sunset, to fill the white honeycombs with nectar and honey, so the women gathered in their wombs the toil of the men.

But doubly clever Zeus proved himself, for he added yet another evil. Should any man manage to evade marriage and reach old age by escaping women, he would find himself without any support in later life. If, on the other hand, he was rich, his property would be divided among distant relatives.

A good wife, wise in soul, can balance evil with good in life. But one who comes across a woman of bad lineage would have lived with unceasing anguish in his chest. This was Zeus' punishment for the entire human race.

4.3 The 12 Labors of Heracles

The first two labors that Eurystheus inflicted on Heracles consisted of killing and skinning the enormous Lion of Nemea, a monster of rather mysterious origins: probably the son of Typhon and Echidna (and, therefore, brother of the Hydra of Lerna), perhaps of Zeus and Selene. The Nemean Lion appeared as a huge beast with claws that cut more than any sword and could not be wounded by iron, bronze, or stone. He became ferocious and would ravage several lands, slaughtering men and herds. This beast would kill anyone it encountered, and its cloak was red from the blood of its victims.

The lion seemed to have a habit of shape-shifting, pretending to be a damsel in distress to attract and maul warriors and heroes.

Heracles headed to where the lion lived, arriving near his den, a cave. He hid himself. Soon after, he saw him coming from far away, all smeared with blood.

Heracles shot several arrows, but all of them bounced off the thick hair. The lion gave a yawn as he licked his lips. Heracles took his sword and swung at it, but the iron curved.

"How can I beat him?" Heracles wondered.

Seeing an olive tree, he built himself a club. Thanks to this, he gave a hard blow on the animal's snout, so that the dazed and stunned lion entered his den with his ears ringing.

Heracles chased him into the cave, beginning a tremendous fight. Finally, he blocked the lion, put his arm under its throat and strangled it.

Zeus, to make the memory of his son's feat eternal, placed the Lion in the sky as a constellation and sign of the Zodiac.

After slaying the hideous beast, the hero tried unsuccessfully to flay it, but nothing could scratch that wonderful skin. But Athena, who had observed his efforts, advised him to use a claw from the beast itself.

Thus, Heracles made a cloak. The skin of the Nemean lion covered his shoulders and the skull of the beast served as his helmet. Heracles took the skin to Eurystheus but the ruler, because of the fear it instilled in him, did not want it. He was so afraid of the power of Heracles and his prey that he holed up in a large jar! He took refuge there whenever Heracles returned from an assignment.

Whenever we see a statue or depiction of a tall, strong man with a club and a lion's skin, we know for sure that it is Heracles.

Heracles obtained a new order: slay the Hydra of Lerna, a nine-headed serpentine beast, daughter of Typhon and Echidna, that haunted and guarded the Lake of Lerna, in whose waters was hidden the gateway to the afterlife.

Hydra was a being so poisonous that it could kill a man with a single breath. The only way to kill it was to cut between its heads the one immortal. To accomplish this task, Heracles was accompanied by his young nephew, Iolaus. Lerna was located near the city of Argos, so they took a chariot and horses and set out. Iolaus began to drive.

When the two arrived, Hydra was in her cave. Heracles forced her out by shooting flaming arrows. He attacked her, holding his breath. Hydra wrapped her feet around him, trying to block him, but Heracles shattered her one, two, three heads with his club.

Heracles was prepared for these difficulties, but not for the fact that for every head cut off, the hideous creature grew back two, thus becoming more and more dangerous. Being in great difficulty, the hero had to enlist the cooperation of his nephew, Iolaus, who, perhaps at Athena's suggestion, set fire to the stumps of the severed heads with a torch, thus preventing their regrowth.

Thus he was able to overcome the no small disadvantage, and despite the intervention of Charcinus, a giant crab sent by Hera to get in the hero's way, Heracles was able to defeat the Hydra. After decapitating her once and for all, he buried her immortal head under a rock and soaked his arrows in her poisonous blood.

Hera wanted to make this faithful animal of hers eternal by placing it in the sky by becoming one of the signs of the Zodiac, Cancer.

However, with the help of Iolaus, Eurystheus refused to consider the evidence valid and sent Heracles toward a third endeavor: to succeed in capturing the Cerynean doe by bringing her back without killing her. It was a large doe sacred to Artemis, the goddess of hunting, with bronze (or brass, depending on the version) hooves and magnificent golden horns, capable of scampering faster than a shot arrow.

As a girl, the goddess had noticed five beautiful, large hinds with golden antlers that shone in the sun and bronze hooves. She had captured four of them by tying them to her chariot. The fifth had escaped but was promised to her. The deer were said to wear a collar with the inscription, "I am consecrated to Artemis."

The main purpose of the ordeal was actually to try to bring down the wrath of Artemis on Heracles for hunting a creature sacred to her. In any case, having chased the doe for a whole year throughout Greece, Thrace, Istria, and the land of the Hyperboreans, and having finally succeeded in catching it (as to how, there are various and divergent versions), Heracles met Artemis and her brother Apollo on the way home and asked for forgiveness for his act. He vowed to return the beast after exhibiting it to Eurystheus. So the goddess handed the deer over to him.

In the company of the doe, Eurystheus demanded that she be taken to his zoo. Realizing that he had to set her free, Heracles agreed on the condition that the ruler take her from his hands. As soon as he let her go, the doe escaped in the blink of an eye, joining her sisters and Artemis. The hero could thus claim that Eurystheus was too slow to catch her.

Increasingly angry at his cousin's successes, Eurystheus, for the fourth effort, sent him to capture the mighty boar Erimantheus, a huge beast sent by Apollo to eliminate Adonis, one of the goddess Aphrodite's favorites, who was responsible for blinding her son Erimantheus, who had observed her bathing.

On his way to the mountain where the animal lived, Heracles first went to Pholus, a longtime centaur friend of his, with whom he shared a meal. When Heracles asked for wine, the centaur regretted that he had only the wine given to him by Dionysus as a gift intended for the centaurs with whom he was supposed to share it. Heracles managed to persuade him by opening the bottle anyway, but when it was opened, the smell drew in all the other centaurs. These, enraged at not being invited to drink the wine with Pholus, attacked Heracles, who was forced to eliminate them with his poisoned arrows. Some of the wounded centaurs died, while the others fled.

Pholus removed the arrow from the body of one of the dead and murmured:

"It is impossible for such a minor injury to have killed such a robust centaur!" He was not aware of Hydra's poison.

Pholus, intrigued by the effectiveness of the arrows, grabbed one but dropped it, injuring himself and being poisoned in turn. At that very instant, the arrow fell from his hand and struck him in the foot. Pholus died. Heracles honored his friend with magnificent and lavish funerals.

One of the arrows also struck the wise centaur Chiron, who had been Heracles' teacher in his youth. The latter, unlike the others, was immortal, but the poison caused him excruciating pains, to the point that he renounced his immortality in favor of Prometheus by taking the latter's place in the punishment inflicted by Zeus for stealing fire from the gods (evidently believing that getting eaten forever liver from an eagle was preferable to the poison of Hydra). The punishment, however, did not last long, as Heracles himself killed the raptor that was tormenting him.

Chiron revealed to the hero that in order to catch the boar, he had to lure the animal and take it into the snow.

The hero then set out in search of the boar. It was winter and snowing. Heracles discovered the animal's den in the middle of the dense forest. He chased the animal until he was able to force the creature into a very narrow snow-filled ditch. Heracles jumped on its back and rode it all the way to Tiryns. Only at the last moment did he put the animal on his shoulders to show it to the ruler Eurystheus - who, of course, had already hidden himself in the pot!

The latter was so frightened that he went and hid in a barrel begging his cousin to dispose of the animal.

A friend of Eurystheus was the ruler Augeas. He had received from his father three hundred black bulls with white legs, two hundred horses with red hair, thousands of other animals, and twelve exceptional white-limbed bulls, which protected the cattle from the attacks of ferocious animals.

The stables, which had not been cleaned for 30 years, were overwhelmed with an immense amount of manure, and huge swarms of flies blurred the view throughout the area. Even the valleys where grazed were covered by a thick layer of manure so high that neither plowing nor planting was possible anymore.

Having agreed with Augeas that he would take care of the cleaning, the latter said that he would be given a tenth of the cattle if he could finish the work in one day. Then he, inspired by Athena, split the walls of the palace, thus diverting the course of the two rivers, the Alpheus and the Peneus, so that they would carry away the dirt, thus freeing the grazing areas. Thus, the waters entered the valley, sweeping away all the dirt. Before long, the waters also cleaned the sheepfolds and the valley of pastures. Eventually, Heracles led the two rivers back to their natural course.

Augean, certain that the hero would fail in his mission, did not willingly accept the outcome and refused to entrust him with the promised cattle, claiming that it was the rivers that cleaned them, not him. For this reason, Heracles eliminated him by delivering the kingdom into the hands of his son, Philo, who had instead sided against his father in preference to Heracles. Eurystheus, however, refused to consider this evidence valid, since Heracles had demanded compensation.

If Hera was the hero's bitter enemy throughout his life, Athena, in contrast, was his most faithful protector. Eurystheus, for the next effort, commissioned the death of the stylophorous birds. First they lived on the Black Sea; later there was an invasion of wolves and the birds fled, settling on Lake Stymphalos.

Stymphalian birds, sacred birds of Ares, lived in the marshes of Lake Stymphos and fed on human flesh. They had bronze beaks, razor-sharp metal feathers (which they were able to hurl at their victims to stab them), and toxic droppings!

Heracles, sent to kill the birds, could not go far enough into the marshes because he did not have enough solid ground on which to move. Athena came to his aid, giving him a bronze rattle specially made by Hephaestus. Heracles climbed onto a rock that was high above the marsh and began to shake the contraption given to him by Athena.

At that sound, the birds began to flutter wildly, and Heracles managed to kill several of them with his arrows. The rest, gathered in a giant flock, headed east, returning to their land on the Black Sea.

Heracles saw them again years later when he headed to those lands with the Argonauts in search of the Golden Fleece. Thus ended the sixth effort.

Eurystheus then commanded Heracles to confront another beast, the Cretan bull, which together with King Minos' wife, Pasiphae, had given rise to the Minotaur, and bring it back to life.

It was a divine bull. Many years before, Minos, the ruler of Crete, stood on the beach and observed the sea. Suddenly, he affirmed:

"Poseidon, I will immolate the first being to emerge from the sea!"

The god made a wonderful white bull with huge lunate horns appear.

As soon as Minos saw him, so extraordinarily beautiful, he did not feel like killing him. He hid it among his beasts, sacrificing another animal instead. This angered Poseidon, who made the bull so aggressive and violent that it ravaged the land, uprooted trees and demolished garden walls.

Arriving in the city, the hero met Minos who, happy to get rid of the animal, allowed him to take it away, even offering his help in catching it. Heracles agreed. Minos informed him that the bull was giving off flames from its nostrils.

Having caught the animal from behind, Heracles grabbed it and strangled it, without killing it, because of its great strength, and then sent it to Eurystheus. The latter, from his safe haven in the barrel where he had thrown himself at the mere sight of the bull, suggested sacrificing the beast to Hera. But the goddess refused the sacrifice on the grounds that, by doing so, Heracles would enjoy reflected glory.

As a result, the bull was released and settled near Marathon, where he would later be kidnapped by Theseus and immolated to Apollo, who intended to emulate the exploits of Heracles.

The next assignment assigned to Heracles was to kidnap the mares of Diomedes, the giant ruler of Thrace and son of Ares.

The mares were to be captured but not killed. They were four gorgeous but fierce animals that belonged to Diomedes of Thrace (not the one from the Trojan War). Such a king was no less violent than his mares as he fed them human flesh, that of his guests or unsuspecting wayfarers.

We also know the names of these mares: Podargos, Lampon, Xanthos and Deimos.

They had never experienced the bit or bridle, but Heracles managed to tame them and tie them to Diomedes' chariot, then set off at great speed. After kidnapping the mares with the help of some of his friends, the hero stayed behind to fight against Diomedes, abandoning his favorite companion Abderus to watch over the mares, who was then devoured by them. In anger, Heracles killed Diomedes, ripped him to shreds by feeding him to his mares, who somehow calmed down, allowing him to be led without too much difficulty to Eurystheus.

According to some versions, the ruler had the beasts sacrificed to Hera. According to others, however, he released them, having now become harmless, near Argos. According to still others, he wished to have them sacrificed to Zeus, who refused them and had them killed by wolves, lions and bears sent by him.

In any case, Heracles had passed this test. The nine labors arose from the bizarre whim of a girl, the young daughter of the ruler Eurystheus.

"Father, I am aware that the queen of the Amazons, Hippolyta, has a beautiful golden belt, well.... I would definitely want it."

Therefore, Heracles was sent for her.

Hippolyta's belt was a gift this queen received from her father, Ares. It represented a symbol of the power she wielded over her people.

The Amazons, the famous women fighters, were experts in horseback riding. They were also brave and very strong in war. They lived on the banks of the Thermodon, a stream that flowed into the Black Sea. The helmets and short tunics they wore were made from the skins of slaughtered animals. If children were born, the Amazons gave them to other tribe. Sometimes they kept them as servants but, as soon as they were born, they would break their arms so that they would remain weak.

Daughters were fed only one breast because the other was amputated so that they could handle weapons more easily. Once they grew up, the girls were trained in combat.

Heracles boarded a 'boat with some companions thus arriving at the port of Themiscyra in the territory of the Amazons.

As of this time, there are various conflicting legends. According to one myth, Queen Hippolyta boarded the ship to welcome the hero. Seeing him, she fell madly in love with him, spontaneously entrusting him with her belt.

Another myth relates that Heracles kidnapped Hippolyta's beloved sister and as she wandered alone in a deserted place proposed an exchange: "I will give you your sister unharmed and you will give me the golden belt."

The third myth states, however, that as soon as he landed, Heracles visited the queen. When he told her why he had come to her country, Hippolyta, perhaps captivated by the handsome hero, was willing to give him her belt. The goddess Hera, however, was unwilling to allow t h e hated Heracles to accomplish his goal so easily. So she disguised herself as an Amazon by going around the city and spreading the word that the Greeks who came with the ship were posing as friends but intended to kidnap the queen.

This rumor was further fueled by the behavior of Theseus, who had escorted Heracles on the journey and then decided to kidnap one of the warriors, Antiope.

At that point, the Amazons attacked the Greeks. Heracles, believing that he had been tricked and that Hippolyta was tricking him, eliminated her by slipping off her belt.

The expedition headed back to Greece, and Heracles gave the fantastic belt to Eurystheus, who wasted no time in sending it off on a new mission.

For the tenth effort, Eurystheus forced Heracles to take possession of the livestock of Geryon, son of Chrysaur and grandson of Medusa, without paying for it or even asking him.

Geryon lived on an island in the far west. The journey was rather long and full of vicissitudes.

Heracles even reached where the lands of Europe, which at that time were said to be connected to Africa, end. He divided the two continents by creating a channel (today called the Strait of Gibraltar). In any case, he raised a column on both sides, with a large inscription, "Non plus ultra," meaning "not go beyond." And for a long time, no navigator dared to cross the Pillars of Heracles.

To reach the island and capture the cattle, Heracles needed a boat, but he could not find one. He remained, therefore, lying on the beach under the scorching sun. Our brave protagonist grabbed an arrow from his quiver and shot it at the sun.

Helium became very angry and asked him, " How dare you?"

"Elio, I made a mistake, but I have a serious inconvenience that nags at me and makes me restless and nervous. I could really use a boat."

"Heracles, I also apologize because I admire your courage, great strength and tenacity, which is why I have decided to help you: I will grant you my cup."

It was a huge golden cup. Every night, when Helius came west with his chariot while it was night, he would climb with the chariot and his four horses onto the cup. Afterwards he would return to the east, passing under the ground. From the east, he would depart again the next day.

Heracles climbed onto the cup and, using the lion's skin as a sail, reached the island.

Arriving at the place where Geryon lived, Heracles saw him being amazed as he was a real monster.

He had three heads and three bodies up to his waist, six arms and only one pair of legs. His faithful and fierce dog Orthrus, brother of Cerberus, had "only" two heads.

The duel was rather short: Heracles eliminated the dog by using two clubs. Then, with a single arrow, he pierced Gerion's three bodies.

He managed to get the herd onto the golden cup and, returning to the mainland, handed the cup back to Helium, thanking him.

On the return journey, Heracles traveled through all the European countries t h a t l a y on the shores of the Mediterranean, arriving even in Latium, where Rome would rise many centuries later.

Evening came and Heracles swam to the Tiber River with the flock. King Evander, delighted to have the famous Heracles in town, received him with all the appropriate honors. Afterwards, Heracles, lay down on the Aventine Hill to rest.

In a cave nearby lived a terrible man named Caucus, who had stolen four cows and four oxen from him by hiding them in a cave. He had in fact dragged the animals by their tails making them walk backwards. Thus the footprints seemed to be heading out of the cave and not in. This ruse deceived Heracles.

Our heroic protagonist was already moving away when the animals bellowed, thus making their presence known.

Heracles found the cave, but a huge boulder was blocking the passage. Thanks to his exceptional strength, he moved it and gave Cauca a blow with his club to the head, bringing back the cattle. According to some versions, he took the cattle back thanks to the support of the thief's sister, Cauca.

A short time later, Hera sent a fly to disturb and disperse the herd, which forced the hero to take an entire year to gather it together by finally handing it over to Eurystheus, who offered the cattle as a sacrifice to Hera after hiding them in the large pot.

Eight years and one month passed. Initially, the hero was very young. Then, little by little, over the years, he became mature.

When Heracles led Jerion's herd back to Eurystheus, thus completing the tenth of the labors required of him, his cousin refused to declare his period of servitude ended, claiming that neither killing the Hydra of Lerna nor cleaning Augea's stables was valid. Therefore, he assigned him two more labors.

The first, of these two last labors, would lead him to the land of the Hesperides, to collect the golden apples that grew in their fantastic garden precisely on the tree around which Ladon, the hundred-headed dragon-snake that never rested, was clinging. Thanks to each of the hundred mouths, he was able to communicate with a different voice each time.

Heracles was not aware of where this garden was located, so during the journey he was forced to ask many people for information, thus traveling great distances.

The person who helped him the most was Prometheus.

"The Garden of the Hesperides is located in the west of Libya, Africa. Nearby lives my brother Atlas. He is the father of the Hesperides; he built the wall of the garden, plus he knows the dragon very well. Let him help you."

According to some versions, in order to find the garden, Heracles went in search of the river and metamorphic god Nereus, who was endowed with omniscience, and imprisoned him, thus succeeding in getting him to reveal the information he needed.

According to still others, Heracles killed Ladon thus taking possession of the apples.

Upon his arrival, Heracles asked for the help of Atlas, the titan father of the Hesperides, who held the sky on his shoulders. Heracles offered to replace him while he went to retrieve the apples. Upon his return, however, Atlas attempted to deceive Heracles by offering to deliver the apples in his place, with the intention of not resuming his post. Heracles pretended to acquiesce, but asked Atlas to hold the sky for a few minutes to allow him to settle the cloak on his shoulders so that he would be more comfortable. When Atlas resumed holding the sky, the hero picked up the apples and left.

It is not clear why Heracles found Atlas in the flesh since his great-grandfather Perseus had turned him into stone out of compassion, using Medusa's head, long before.

When Eurystheus saw the apples, he dared not guard them since they were divine. Heracles then handed them over to Athena, who brought them back to the Garden of the Hesperides.

The last task Heracles faced was conceived as the most arduous. He was sent to the underworld to track down and capture Cerberus, son of Typhon and Echidna, who prevented the escape of souls from the underworld. It was a dog with three heads full of snakes and a tail full of quills.

Once he entered the underworld, Heracles struggled a bit to convince the ferryman Charon to lead him into the Acheron. And once he got on board, the boat almost sank under his weight, since he normally led only shadows.

Heracles, in the midst of the dead, had a memorable encounter. He glimpsed the shadow of Meleager, prince of Calydon, who held him and in a moved voice, told him of his tragic and most recent death. He said to Heracles:

"I am distressed at the thought of having left my sister Deianira alone and helpless. Now that I am dead, who will look after her?"

Heracles reassured him, saying:

"When I return to the world of the living, I will go to Calidone and ask for her hand."

Once in the realm of the dead, he met his ancient companions, Theseus and Pyrito, imprisoned there for attempting to kidnap Hades' wife Persephone. After a partially successful attempt to free them (Pyrite's desire for a god's wife was too severe to allow him to be freed), the hero went to Hades to ask permission to bring Cerberus to the surface. The god granted it on the condition that he proved capable of defeating the monstrous dog without using weapons, which Heracles was happy to do.

Heracles grabbed Cerberus by the throat. The dog tried to strike him with snakes and spines, but the indestructible skin of the Nemean Lion defended him. So the hero, after grasping him, did not let go until, by now half-drowned, Cerberus had to resign himself.

At this point Hermes Psychopompus, a helper of Charon, who knew the Underworld very well and was able to bring Heracles and the hideous beast out of the realm of the dead, took over.

As soon as he saw the light, Cerberus became frightened and began to bark angrily with his three mouths. The saliva falling on the lawn caused wolfsbane, a very toxic herb, to grow. When Eurystheus received the "delivery," he affirmed:

"Heracles, I saw, it's okay, now you can lead the beast back to Hades. You have finished your purification, now you are free!"

4.4 Eros and Psyche

Once upon a time in a city there lived a king and queen who had three beautiful daughters. The two older daughters, although pretty, enjoyed ordinary beauty and both were married. The third daughter, whose name was Psyche, was so beautiful that rumors spread that she was the goddess Aphrodite herself, which was not true, thus attributing divine honors to her. Aphrodite despised the girl for this reason she called young Eros to report. Pointing Psyche out to him, the goddess commanded, "Eros, you must make Psyche fall in love with the most unpleasant and unhappy of men!"

But when Eros saw the girl, he fell madly in love with her. Remarkably, the one who fell in love was the one who first, thanks to his magic bow, made gods and men fall in love. In the meantime, Psyche's father began to worry since this daughter, admired and revered by almost everyone, had no suitors, risking, therefore, not getting married. He therefore took her with him to seek advice from the oracle. The answer was terrible: "Psyche must be taken to the top of a mountain, dressed as a bride. A huge winged monster, feared even by the father of the gods Zeus, will come for her." All the inhabitants took the girl to the top of a mountain, who, left alone, fell asleep. When she awoke, she found herself in a grove near a spring spotting a strange building. She entered it, but it was deserted, with only voices and invisible hands acquiescing to her every desire. During the night, in complete darkness, the groom entered her bed and slept with her. And so on the following nights. He made her promise, "Never try to see me or understand who I may be." Psyche, however, was happy because she loved her husband and in turn felt loved.

Much time passed since then. Her sisters, who were envious of Psyche's fate, visited her and persuaded her to try to find out who her husband was, who, according to legend was supposed to be a hideous monster. Psyche tried to resist her curiosity, but she could not repress her desire to see her husband's face for long. One night, in fact, while her husband was sleeping, she took a lamp and approached the bed. Psyche saw that it was not a monster, but a beautiful boy.

She bent down to kiss him and a drop of boiling oil fell from the lamp onto Eros's shoulder. He suddenly woke up exclaiming, "Now you have seen me. I am the messenger of love, the god Eros. I disobeyed Aphrodite's order to make you fall in love with an unpleasant and poor man, for I myself fell in love with you. But you did not fulfill your promise. You wanted to know my true identity, so by doing so you will never see me again." Then he flew away.

Psyche, devastated, initially attempted to commit suicide by throwing herself into a river. However, the river god himself supported her by gently laying her on a meadow. She wandered the moors in search of her lost love until she reached the temple of Aphrodite. There, she asked for forgiveness. Aphrodite revealed herself, but she was still furious with Psyche for joining her son.

Now, the only thing Aphrodite wanted was for Psyche to suffer. She told Psyche that perhaps she could re-embrace Eros after passing some tests. Aphrodite ordered the girl to put a large amount of grain in order by evening. The young woman was in despair. She was unable to obey Aphrodite's order, but compassionate ants emerged by the thousands from the bowels of the earth to help her by doing all the work for her.

Once she returned, Aphrodite found the various grains in order. She went into a rage and ordered Psyche to get some golden wool from special sheep. Psyche approached them, but a farmer's staff stopped her, warning her that if she wanted to approach the sheep she would have to wait until they were asleep first. Then she could approach the brambles, where large tufts of golden wool were entangled, pick them up and take them to Aphrodite.

Psyche completed her second task and even a third where she was asked to fetch water from a spring impassable and inaccessible. Psyche was able to pass this test with the help of an eagle. Anyone was willing to help the young woman. As a final test, Aphrodite ordered her, " Go down to the Underworld and ask Persephone for her special and mysterious bottle." Aphrodite happened to forget to warn Psyche of a very important detail: to get to the underworld, first, one had to die.

Psyche, in despair, was about to throw herself off a tower when the tower itself spoke magically to her, showing her how to reach the underworld safely. Psyche therefore descended into the underworld and there sniffed the bottle. She fell into an eternal sleep. She would have remained forever in the underworld if Eros had not rushed to her aid and rescued her and brought her back to earth. Psyche remained asleep for a long time until Eros, unhappy since he was unable to forget her, awakened her, wounding her with a small arrow. In fact he had always been with her in the form of ants, farmer, eagle and talking tower. He had always been by her side helping her through each of the trials. Later, Eros asked Zeus for permission to take his bride to Olympus. There, Psyche made her peace with Aphrodite. She ate ambrosia, drank the nectar and, in this way, became immortal. From the union of Eros and Psyche a child named Hedone was born.

4.5 Apollo and Daphne

Daphne, daughter and priestess of Gaia, Mother Earth and mother of the river Peneus (or, according to others, the river Lacone), was a very young nymph who lived her existence in a carefree manner. She spent her time enjoying the quiet of the woods and the pleasure of hunting. Her life was disrupted by the whim of two deities-Apollo and Eros. Legend has it that one day Apollo, proud of having killed the giant serpent Python with arrows, met Eros, intent on forging a new bow. Apollo began to sneer at Eros since the latter had never performed any memorable deeds. The god of love, deeply hurt by Apollo's words, flew to the top of Mount Parnassus thus preparing his revenge. He took two arrows, one blunt and leaden, intended to repel love, which he shot into Daphne's heart, and another, well-sharpened and golden, intended to bring forth passion, which flew violently into Apollo's heart. From that day on, Apollo began to wander frantically through the woods in search of the nymph, for the passion that harbored in his heart was so strong that every minute away from her represented terrible suffering. Finally, he managed to track her down but, as soon as Daphne saw him, she ran away frightened, and to no avail were the pleas of the god who shouted out his love and divine origins in an attempt to astonish the young maiden. Daphne, frightened, fled into the woods. Realizing, however, that her race proved to be in vain, as Apollo drew nearer and nearer, she invoked the help of Mother Earth. She, pitied by her daughter's pleas, began to transform her body: her hair changed into leafy branches; her arms rose toward the sky, becoming flexible branches; her sinuous body became covered with tender bark; her delicate feet became strong roots, and her delicate face disappeared among the branches of the trees. Daphne had transformed into a graceful and strong laurel tree that took the name Laurus. The transformation had taken place under the eyes of Apollo, who, in despair, embraced the trunk in the hope of finding sweet Daphne again. Ovid writes in the Metamorphoses, "Apollo was in love with her; he wrapped the plant as if it were the body of the nymph; he kissed the branches as if they were arms, but the tree seemed to rebel against those kisses. Then the disappointed god said to her, "Since you cannot be my bride, you will at least be my tree: my hair, my harp, my quiver will always be decorated by you. The god loudly announced, therefore, that the laurel tree would become sacred and most important for his worship. A sign of glory to be placed on the heads of the victors. That is why even today, in memory of Daphne, it is customary to encircle the heads of those who accomplish memorable feats with a laurel wreath.

www.ingramcontent.com/pod-product-compliance
Lightning Source LLC
Chambersburg PA
CBHW071459080526
44587CB00014B/2158